~ SMIRK ~

A COMPILATION OF
HUMOR COLUMNS AND CARTOONS

For Terrence,
one of the Best writers
I know, Thanks for
guiding me in my
own writing,
Carol

CAROL NELSON FALCONE

outskirtspress
DENVER, COLORADO

DEDICATION:

To my loving Family
Especially my wonderful parents
Ron & Judy Nelson
and my amazing siblings, Steven, Robert & Amy and their families.
Thank you all for your love and support through-out the years.

~ ~ ~ ~ ~ ~ ~ ~ ~ ~ ~ ~ ~ ~

I'd like to thank my college professor from SUNY Fredonia
Dr. Karen Mills-Courts
For inspiring me to write and giving me the tools to do it.

~ ~ ~ ~ ~ ~ ~ ~ ~ ~ ~ ~ ~ ~

The following people need to be recognized for their inspiration in my life:
Matthew Hattley, Maggie Andreasen, Fred Falcone, Kathy Green, Paul Punsal, Sue Liebe,
Valerie Nightingale, Cyndi Wright, Nancy Bertrand-Loesch, Rachel Hirsch, Edward Huether,
Michael Grunsky, Billy & Barbara Reilly, Kenny & Diane Reilly, Morning Bird Jackson, Bob
Osterhoudt, Tonya Hughes, Cathy Gross, Michelle Fournier, Nicole Golubeff, Karla Thomas, Andrea
DiDinato, Roger Baker, The Shawangunk Journal, And the Ya-Ya's (Pat, Shirley, Charlotte, and
Rosemary)

~ ~ ~ ~ ~ ~ ~ ~ ~ ~ ~ ~ ~ ~

And most especially this book is for my incredible children
~ Zoe & Lucca ~
Mommy loves you so very much!

~ ~ ~ ~ ~ ~ ~ ~ ~ ~ ~ ~ ~ ~

Thank you, God, for making this happen.

TABLE OF CONTENTS

~ Chapter One ~
Relationship Handicapped

~ Chapter Two ~
Domestication is the 7th Ring of Dante's Inferno

~ Chapter Three ~
'Tis the Season....

~ Chapter Four ~
The Family that Stays together get's Awfully Squirelly

~ Chapter Five ~
Random thoughts of a Mid-Life Meltdown

~ Chapter Six ~
The Daily Grind

~ CHAPTER ONE ~
RELATIONSHIP HANDICAPPED

As most of life seems to revolve around the up's and down's of romance I figured it was as good a place as any to start. Lord knows I've had the rockiest of love lives after being left at the altar THREE times. I honestly think I should be eligible for some sort of handicapped benefits for that. The end result of such a slap stick romantic existence is the annoyance of constantly thinking, "Could it be, me?"

~ DATING NIGHTMARES ~

I'm typically what I'd like to refer to as "dating impaired", or "relationship handicapped." I should have my own handicapped parking space at the mall for cryin' out loud! The sign would be a picture of a happy couple with a red circle and line through it. If there were a kingdom entitled "Blind Date Land" or "On-line Dating Country" I would undeniably be the Queen of both. I have been set-up with more lunatics than anyone else on the planet. My expertise lies in the poor hygiene/cross-dressing/psychotic category.

Let's start with hygiene horrors and then we'll deal with transvestites and psychotics. My latest string of dates have had really unacceptable grooming methods. Unfortunately for me I'm not a shallow person. The last person I dated I nicknamed "B.O. Man". His tag line, like a cartoon with trumpets blaring, would be "Able to blow anyone away in a single raise of his arm! Yes, it's *B.O Man* - the man without deodorant!" It was so incredibly bad that my friends would hurt themselves trying to get the car windows down as quickly as possible. The first few dates I tried to get up the nerve to talk to him about it but how do you tell someone they stink? So I found this "natural deodorant rock" in the health food store (what I go through for male companionship) and started a casual conversation. "I just found this neat little thing — it's a rock that you use as a deodorant." Then he says, "I don't like to use anything and showering dries my skin out." I just snapped at that point, and blurted out "You need to do something, buddy, my cat's even turning green for God sakes!" Yeah, it pretty much ended right there.

The next guy I dated we'll just call, "Booger Boy." Just picture this — I'm making a nice gourmet meal for the guy and casually enjoying wine, he's across the counter from me and I'm looking him straight in the eyes, when midway through my sentence he picks his nose right dead in front of me! I'm so shocked I start to stumble over my words and an atomic mushroom cloud is going off in my brain. Before I can think of something to say he does one of those "roll-it-between-his-index-finger-and-thumb-flinging-it-on-the-wall-routines." My mind was just blown. I actually started to think I imagined it because no sane person would ever do that. I mean I was *looking right at him* when he did it. After that he used my bathroom and left the toilet seat up and I figured if he did all this in just a few dates, then it can only go even further downhill from there.

Don't even get me started on "Timmy the Transvestite" who probably was the inspiration for the Rocky Horror Picture Show. One day he was meeting me at my house. I ran late, he found the key under the mat, the equation adds up to me kicking open my bedroom door to find him standing there, all dolled up putting in bright red lipstick, wearing a corset, garters, black fishnet stockings and **white** high heels. Once again, the atomic mushroom cloud went off in my head. I mean, what the hell do you say in a situation like this? How do you respond? Coming home to see your date dressed like a whore defies all emotional boundaries. Maybe it was the shock to my system but I swear to you the only thing that I could think of to say was: "You don't wear white shoes after Labor Day and honestly, with black fishnet stockings, is just plain tacky."

The worst part is that people started thinking "I" have a problem because I break up with what they see as nice men. "Carol Ann, why don't you go out with Rose's son, he's a lawyer, 38, nice, and he's catholic too." "Ma, I'm still working on getting the basics down! If he showers, uses deodorant, doesn't pick his nose, puts the toilet seat down and doesn't wear my lipstick I'd be happy." Well, turns out Rose's son wore crazy shoes if you know what I mean. One word of advice — don't bring up that you regularly see flying saucers on your first date. He says, after 10 minutes into a cup of cappuccino, "So I was barbecuing on my back porch the other day and a UFO came flying by." ~Sigh~ Why, Lord, Why???

~ VALENTINE'S DAY SHOULD BE CALLED "ANTI-SINGLE'S DAY" ~

I like to affectionately call Valentine's Day, "Anti-Single's Day" since it's biased against anyone that's not part of a couple. I really hate this day with a passion. "V-Day" rhymes with "D-Day" with a capital "D," which stands for "Doom." Every Valentine's Day, like some sick unearthly joke, I am forced to fight the clutches of death. For the majority of Valentine's Days past I have had various attempts by God to remove me from the planet on *that day*! Isn't that odd? The most romantic day of the year and bad things happen. It's an omen. It's bad enough I have to deal with a stinking holiday that rubs my own loveless life back in my face but I also have to fight mortality as well.

I have a list of all the things that went wrong for me on numerous Valentine's Days, such as: getting run over by a bus, being robbed at gun-point, driving off a cliff, having food poisoning, accidentally setting my hair on fire (yup, completely bald), and then, my personal favorite — appendix rupturing and dying on the operating table (nope, didn't see any white light … not a good sign). Then there was the year that the house got robbed; the following year it would catch fire and burn down. And then there was the Valentine's Day I spent in the hospital after my mother got into a car accident; the following year I got into a car accident, then the dog died, got struck by lightning, left in a foreign country without any identification, and so on. Seriously, what are the chances of these events happening on the same day each year? If it didn't happen to *me* I wouldn't believe it myself. Every V-day is cause for sheer terror in Carol-world.

I finally started to get the message loud and clear when I met this guy, "Nick," early February one year. Sure enough, my personal favorite holiday of death rolls around and so I decide to go out and try not to be depressed. Lo and behold, I see Nick at a party and worked up enough nerve to talk to him. Things seemed to be going well and I actually foolishly thought that I might escape the date unscathed. We got to talking and he said he was a musician.

"Guess what instrument I play," he said.

So I'm being all flirty trying to guess, "Ummm, piano? Harp? Saxophone?"

Suddenly he's looking more and more furious. He holds his left hand up and angrily growls, "*drums*!" Wouldn't you know it – he was missing his *wedding*-ring finger. It was gone. Oh, was it ever gone. It was just soooo not there. How the hell I didn't notice the man didn't have a finger I have no idea. And here I was guessing all these instruments that required all your fingers to be present. He thought I was making fun of him. If that isn't indicative of my life, I don't know what is. What are the chances that of all the men I will meet on Valentine's Day it's a man missing his ring finger? It was a sarcastic joke from God in the form of symbolism to let me know I will be alone, man-less, for all eternity till my womb dries up and falls out like a bitter crusty prune. You know, in Shakespearian times they believed it was a sin for a woman to not have a man and her special punishment was leading apes around hell by a leash after she died. For me I'm sure they'll make an exception, won't they? Maybe I can get away with just a Chihuahua.

I was married on Valentine's Day to my first husband. He spontaneously decided that we should just take the plunge and go to a justice of the peace and get married on Valentine's Day after I explained my bad luck with this day. He said he wanted to forever change my luck with this day and make it our wedding anniversary. Two months later he left me for my best friend and cleaned out my bank account. I'm cursed!

So I wonder what will happen this year. Will I be struck by a delivery truck carrying heart-shaped candies that say, "hot stuff"? Will *Match.com* decline my membership? Will I get a bouquet of wrenches from a secret admirer? Actually that's not so bad. One year I got a stainless steel "snake" for the toilet bowl. How romantic is that? I hear they're having an "Anti-Valentine's Day Parade" in New York City this year. I might as well grab a leash and lead King Kong down past Macy's walking side by side for all flippin' eternity.

~ "FORGET YOU, AND FORGET HER TOO!" ~

I am positively the proud owner of the hellish break-up award. Unfortunately, this is something that is universal — everyone goes through a bad break-up now and then. And as the saying goes, misery loves company so I'll go first.

Most romantic relationships don't end good. Think about it — if it ended "good" then why would there be a need to end it at all? The only thing that ends good is a movie. Every once in awhile former lovers agree to disagree, part ways peacefully and go their separate ways without bloodshed. Unfortunately it's more typical that break-up's come complete with angry texts and screaming meltdowns that could get you a booking on a reality show.

It's all good in the beginning when everything's lovey-dovey sunshine filled with rainbows and butterflies, but then somewhere along the line things shift to a rollercoaster ride that jumps the tracks and plummets into a concession stand that makes only fish-flavored milkshakes. The end is like Satan ripping out your heart and feeding it to his minions to eat in front of you with a side of turnips.

Everyone has a flaw and mine happens to be picking men that are completely wrong for me and… well… anybody else. The complete nutball dregs of society seem to be what I'm most attracted to. I sarcastically joke of being dating impaired and unable to distinguish the psychologically twisted mind lurking beneath the surface of your common Joe-Shmo. They all look totally normal walking down the street but then, like a stray dog, you take him home only to discover they will pee on your bed, wreck your house, give you fleas, and have a hang-up for some former owner the poor dog just can't shake.

I've come across the most delusional men on this planet. I've dated men that were pathological liars, serial cheaters, bi-polar stalkers, (sometimes all three at once), as well as misogynists, narcissists, emotionally unstable religious fanatics, commitment-phobes, a closet transvestite here and there, a slew of manic depressives and control freaks, and one wife beater in a pear tree. I have been the conductor on the "Relationship Handicapped Train" for a couple decades now and it's a wonder that Stephen King hasn't asked for the rights to my horrific love stories yet. It's time to get off this trippy Disney World ride gone awry because this is one small world I don't want to be exploring anymore.

There are so many types I can barely scratch the surface… men that are so shallow that if you gain one pound they call you fat right in the middle of sex (yeah, I dated some real assholes)... the slew of men who are 47 years old and still living with their mommies... oh and let's not forget the jealous control freaks who have a major melt-down about where you were and who were you with and yadda yadda -- just get some professional help, pal.

It's the "players", though, the serial cheaters with their pathological lying, that truly have no soul. The emotional trauma they inflict on innocent women should be a crime, with a minimum sentence of 10 years in state prison. Let them go without some booty for a decade and seriously think about the bullshit they put their victims through — they'll be good little boys treating their woman like a queen after that, guaranteed. Bring back the Scarlet Letter I say!

Shall we talk about the way the dumping goes? The ones that are truly heartless cowards get caught in the sack with your best friend, write you a "Dear John" on a post-it note, text it, e-mail it, or disappear altogether changing their phone number/e-mail/social accounts without a single word, leaving you wondering what the hell happened.

If you have a real winner on your hands they'll try to convince you that somehow their lying and cheating was all your fault.. or that you made it up somehow. "No, honey, that wasn't your friend, Sheila, jumping outta our bed and through the window butt nekkid — you must be seein' things." Nobody man's up and says, "Ya know, you're right, I'm a schmuck. I wouldn't want to be with me either."

My last man broke up with me last week in the most cowardly of ways — via a harsh text message — while he knew I'd be driving around the hairpin turns of the Shawangunk mountains on my way to work. Hmmm… maybe he was hoping I'd drive off the cliff? So uncouth – he's the type that would wear sweatpants to a funeral. He fit into the lying, cheating, can't get over his ex category. I actually catch him sleeping with another woman and somehow he twisted it around to be my fault. Can ya' believe that crap?

Some of the most famous artists, writers and musicians out there became filthy rich talking about the pain and suffering their exes caused them. Where would we be without the angry break-up album, "Jagged Little Pill" by Alanis Morrissette, or Grammy award winner Adele's "21" CD making a fool of her ex? Who could forget Carrie Underwood singing about slashing her name into her ex's leather truck seats? And just about every time Taylor Swift goes through a romantic break-up she sings about it and gets a Grammy it seems.

Maybe someday that will be me, and all these heartbreaks will not be in vain as I laugh my way to the bank. Until then I'll be in the garage cleaning out the cat litter box that was lined with his favorite Patriot's Jersey that he accidentally left behind, and mumbling to the walls about how the flowers he brought me lasted longer than he did.

~ FIANCÉ #1, FIANCÉ #2, FIANCÉ #3 ~

Yes, that's right – you heard it right – I've been engaged three times and pretty much got "left at the altar" so to speak whether it was the actual day of the wedding or a week prior. Quite frankly I'm surprised it hasn't killed me but since I've been procrastinating writing this chapter it may just kill me yet having to write about it all. This is all true to the best of my knowledge but some parts are a bit fuzzy as I've pretty much utilized the coping skills that wine and sarcasm can provide, in an effort to make fun of the oddity of it all with twisted humor many folk won't get. Either way you will undeniably, react with a "Hell, no, that did not happen to you", "Shut the front door", "OMG, that's totally messed up", or at the very least a "Damn, you poor thing!" Quite honestly I wouldn't of believed it myself if I didn't live it. After the third one I just looked up to the heavens with a "no you didn't" attitude and yelled to the Lord, "Really?!"

Can you imagine having ONE failed wedding let alone THREE, where you were humiliatingly dumped just as you were trying on your dress and the cake was being picked up and all the relatives were dolled up only to discover your groom just ran away with the girl that did his shirts at the dry cleaners? Imagine the horror of having to call hundreds of people to tell them the wedding is off having to repeat the horror of it all over and over again. By the 200th phone call you pretty much lose it.

So wrap that shit all up – the lost deposits, the cost of the dress, the flowers, the whole shebang – now multiply that by THREE. Three men, three weddings planned, dumped at the last minute – what the fuck are the chances of that happening to one woman? I mean one is a rarity and two failed engagements you definitely get concerned, but THREE times? **What are the chances of that happening?**! I mean, shit, at this point, I'm startin' to think it may be "me". .... (thoughtful pause here)...... Nah.... It can't be me – I'm the most sane person in my family... although that ain't sayin' much after you find out about them upon further reading. I've analyzed this whole romantic catastrophe that's fallen upon me and think that either I am really, really, really, really bad at picking men, God hates me, or it's a gypsy curse. I'm bettin' on gypsy curse.

What truly sucked was having to return all those wedding gifts to everyone. I'm pretty sure by the last engagement my relatives re-gifted me the same crap they gave me for the previous two. In one of them I found the card addressed to me and the previous groom's name.

Dresses you say? I have enough wedding dresses and bridesmaid dresses in my closet to open my own flippin' boutique! I really felt bad for all my girlfriends because they kept forking over hundreds of dollars each time on dresses they never even wore once. By the last time I said I was getting married they scattered like roaches to the farthest ends of the planet.

How could this happen you may ask. Unfortunately I have a weakness for the charming skirt chasers falling for their devilish good looks and empty promises of love. My mother says I fall for the wolf in sheep's clothing but really I know it's that I go for that motorcycle ridin' bad boy wolf looking for that angelic inner sheep inside him. As you can see it hasn't worked real well for me since I've found wolves are wolves to the core and this little red riding hood just keeps gettin' bit. Got a rabid addiction to bad boy assholes that I just can't seem to shake I guess.

Let's start with Fiancé #1 and give you the low down on that unemployed, redneck winner with less than an ounce of brains. To all the young men out there thinking of proposing to your lady love, under no circumstances should you ever get her diamond ring from "Rent-A-Center" like this idiot did. Imagine my horror when things were already on the rocks for us and there's a knock at the door from the Repo Man looking to reposess the symbol of our love because he lapsed on the payments. Was he trying to cover his ass in case the relationship didn't work out?! Maybe he was figurin' he could return it, no problem, since he was renting it like a widescreen TV on a monthly basis in his double wide. Ain't that a hoot! A rented marriage is what that is - If you don't get along you can return your relationship within 30 days no questions asked, minus the dings and scratches here and there. So nice to know he valued his future wife as much as he did his rented Sony.

Now Fiancé #2 was the slick used car salesman as slimy as they come that wined and dined me, buying me boatloads of lavish gifts - which was refreshing after years of going through the drive-thru was considered a night out on the town. Unfortunately he had a very unnatural relationship with his mother to say the least, had ties to the mob, hated my mother and fought with my father over my wedding dress tearing it to pieces. Shit hit the fan just days before the wedding when he decided to clean out my bank account and run away with that whore at the dry cleaners. Every last cent - all the wedding money, the deposit to the new apartment we were moving into, the honeymoon money – even my paycheck that I just deposited the day before. I didn't even have 50 cents on me to get through the toll to my parent's house with all my belongings in the back of the car and begged the attendant to let me through. So flippin' pathetic, I know, right?! Oy, the stories I could tell you.

Once again had to call all the relatives and return all the gifts and felt so bad I paid back all the bridesmaids the cost of their dresses. I made a mental note to not have so many bridesmaids at the next go round just in case it happened again. It's just hysterical that most bridesmaids bitch about the cost of the dress stating that they only get to wear it once and that's it. Well, hell, if you're in my wedding party you apparently don't even get to wear it once. I remember laughing at that moment thinking there's just no way in hell that it could possibly happen a third time to one woman – that would be absolutely impossible; just absurd! Shit, (LOL), guess I was wrong about that one.

Now when Fiance #3 came around I definitely was in over my head because I obviously had to fess up to my past romantic problems to him and be honest about it and he musta' thought it was not a half bad way to leave your lover and jumped on the bandwagon as well. By this time I'm sure as shit I'm in some weird ass episode of "Candid Camera", "Punk'd", or some sort of messed up "This is your @#$% UP Life Game Show" or something because this shit just doesn't keep happening to the same person.

Fiance # 3 was a rapper dude, eight years younger than me, and after two weeks of crazy funky love decided to get engaged and once again a wedding was planned. The dress was great, the reception romantic, and only two bridesmaids this time (thank God). Unfortunately it was like the Hatfield's and McCoy's with both of our parents getting into horrid screaming matches. He was the typical Mama's boy and she wasn't ready to let go and let him get married and my father felt that she was just a horrible shrew of a woman and forbade her from attending the wedding. The end result was he left me the week before the wedding with my best friend and moved to Albany. Apparently they were having a great old time behind my back for quite some time. What a great gal pal I had there, right?! I'm sure his mother was very happy to hear that and somehow patted herself on the back for being such a wonderful mother instilling good solid beliefs in her fine son. To this day I can never go to Lake George for fear that this Monster-in-law from hell would somehow still be there lurking in her cave waiting to gobble me up.

By the time my ex-husband proposed to me years later I sneered sarcastically, "Yeah, okay, pal, we'll see if you show up," and honestly didn't take any of it seriously until I saw him at the end of the aisle. I showed up a half hour late in a black hummer ready to go to Marriage War in white lace …and … he was still there. What a shocker!

~ MY HONEYMOON
WITH MY SISTER ~

After all the prepping and planning for a year on every detail of your wedding the reward for all that hard work is "the Honeymoon". A time to unwind, relax and bask in the love you just celebrated with your new mate in the most sacred of commitments. At just about every honeymoon resort out there all you'll see is starry-eyed romantic saps all flush with happiness. That is, of course, unless you happen to be "me". I had to take my honeymoon with my sister! God, it was the most pathetic thing ever.

With Fiance #2 I had un-refundable tickets to St. Martin at a honeymoon resort. I was so heart-broken and devastated I didn't want to go but my sister convinced me it would be good to get away; she would go with me and we'd have fun she said. So we headed off with high hopes in an effort to mend my heart and forget all about my run-away groom.

The place wasn't half bad at first glance but looking back there were clues that this wasn't going to be the best idea. The weather was gorgeous, the palm trees luscious, and the waters crystal clear. I put sunscreen on, had a pina colada and fell asleep pool-side next to my sister in the lounge chairs.

Well apparently my sunscreen was too old and lost all ability to protect me and I wound up with third degree burns. The amount of pain I was in could only be described as having your skin ripped off and then lighting yourself on fire. I was flippin' purple for God Sakes… I just put on a moo-moo going completely commando because I couldn't bend over to get a pair of drawers on but I'm sure it would have cut into my blood red skin like salt in the wound anyways. So there I was – first day out – with skin poisoning. Try staying out of the sun on a tropical island for the rest of your vacation. Ugh.

By then everyone else around us assumed we were a lesbian couple that just tied the knot and we had to keep telling people we were sisters, and then they'd want to know why we were at a honeymoon resort, and yadda yadda had to tell the "leaving me at the altar story" and that just made me want to kill myself pretty much. There weren't even any available single men to hit on in an attempt to cheer me up since we were surrounded by newlyweds. Flippin' torture.

But I was still determined to have fun as we sat down to dinner that first night. We filled our plates at the buffet and were about to finally exhale and enjoy ourselves when the lounge singer started his thang. In broken English and a horrible accent that cheesy man on his electric organ belted out the worst version of "Endless Love" I've ever heard (and I hate that song to begin with!) Having to listen to it as a jilted bride though, made me just shake my head with a blank stare at my sister. By the end of the week hearing him sing that same song, every night at the same time I finally lost my appetite. "C'mon, screw dinner, let's get a 6-pack and go back to the room, sis."

Giving up dinner was probably just as well since they served the same exact food items on the lunch and dinner buffets every flippin' day of the week. I went to a fancy resort to eat left-over's on a daily basis. Woo Hoo. I can do that at home.

My sister tried like hell to perk me up. "C'mon, let's get our hair corn-rowed by the ladies on the beach; my treat," she says. "Fine," I grumpily say. So we go down to the beach where the native women have folding chairs set up with a bag of beads braiding the tourist's hair. My sister sits down and gets hers done and with her long blond tresses looks like Bo Derek in "10". So now it's my turn and she's filming me getting it done. The nice lady had me hold her bag of beads and hand her one every few seconds as she pulled on my hair tight as nails. She's got half my head done when someone yells, "Policia" and all those ladies doing braids ran like hell down the beach amidst beads flying everywhere and shouting crap in Spanish. All my sister did was film it while sarcastically singing, "Bad Boys, Bad Boys, watcha' gonna do when they come for you, Bad Boys, Bad Boys!" Apparently it was illegal to braid hair for money and they were rounded up in the paddy wagon. I kept waiting for her to come back and do the other half of my hair but she didn't and I looked like an idiot since I couldn't get the braids and beads out of the one half and had a frizzed afro on the other. The horror.

Then on the way to dinner looking like a burnt troll doll with half its head twisted up like a pretzel, a little native boy came up to me and grasped my hand. I was touched for a moment and then he chomped my finger and almost took a chunk out of me. So after we found a bandage, lived through "Endless Love" again, and once again took a 6-pack back to the room, a little orphaned dog followed us back to our room. We gave him a cracker. Yeah, that was a mistake - he camped out by our door whimpering for the rest of the trip. I didn't see him on the last day and wondered if he would be on the buffet for lunch disguised as fried conch meat.

I haven't even gotten to the good point yet – the crème de la crème of this horrid little tale. For one last fleeting attempt to try to turn this catastrophe of a honeymoon around and salvage this we went out to the gorgeous blue lagoon to do some early morning swimming …topless. We figured that there weren't a lot of people in this area; we're in the Caribbean so who cares kinda attitude. Go with the flow and let your hair down and your ta-ta's loose.

Suddenly my sister sees something dark in the water and points it out to me saying, "What's that over there?" I tell her it's just a patch of seaweed. She slowly starts to move behind me saying, "Yeah, well that seaweed is moving at a pretty fast clip there." With that she leaves me there to get the brunt of whatever is quickly coming straight for us, and pushes some woman off her little rubber raft in a hostile take-over. I was frozen, standing there topless with a sting ray coming right for me, and now my sister was screaming and getting everyone's attention. I believe a tourist from Jersey filmed it and put it on U-Tube.

By the end of the week when we walked out on the lounge act I was so cranky I purposefully knocked over the fire-eater that was walking on glass. I know that's terrible. All I heard was "ahhhh" and a thud and people running and I didn't look back – just kept walking with my beer and bad ass attitude. I vaguely remember yelling to all the stunned honeymooning couples, "Love blows, bitches! You'll all be divorced in five years!"

God, what a horrible nightmare that was – can you imagine living through that? Getting left at the altar to have to take your honeymoon with your sister and it goes completely awry?! Lord, the years of therapy working that one out…

~ CHAPTER TWO ~

DOMESTICATION IS THE 7TH RING OF DANTE'S INFERNO

Oh the joys of settling down and having children and trying to keep your home and yourself in one piece. This section touches on all the stuff that may drive you crazy in domestic life that lead to funny stories to tell your friends ... several times ....preferably over a glass of wine.. Misery loves company afterall.

~ THE MULTI-TASKING JUGGLING ACT ~

Multitasking has come to define our hectic world as being absolutely necessary in order to accomplish all the tasks we've set for ourselves in a typical day. It's amazing how we work 8-12 hours at stressful jobs, schlepping kids around to various sports and activities, keeping the home running smoothly with cooked meals and clean clothes and all the other little obstacles thrown at us on a daily basis. "There's just not enough time in the day to do it all," you find yourself saying to the wall, shaking your head.

It always seems like there's too much on your plate so you're FORCED to do more than one thing at the same time to fit it all in. Hence the term "multi-tasking" has begun to go viral in our society. I would remember my mom was like an octopus with eight arms doing a thousand things at once. I would put my foot over the front seat in the car and ask her to tie my shoe while she drove the car, smoked a cigarette, and put her mascara on. And she'd do it too…. all while teasing her hair to the moon in a cloud of aerosol hairspray while we jumped around the station wagon like screaming hellions (seatbelts were "optional" back then).

Scientists believe that after years of testing the results show that females are better than males at multi-tasking because they're able to reflect upon a problem, while continuing to juggle their other commitments. What's interesting is these really smart scientist guys are stumped as to why and offer no explanation. I say it's because women don't have much of a choice when the baby's screaming holy hell, the dinner's burning in the kitchen, the police are at the front door with her teenaged son, as the sound of a chainsaw and her husband screaming echo's through the neighborhood. All hell is breaking loose – did they think we would suddenly say, "Yeah, I'm gonna go take a bubble bath right about now". Truth be told when cookies come to cookies the only thing being screamed in an emergency is usually, "Maaaaaaaa!!!!"

Sometimes, however, trying to juggle it all will eventually lead to something going kaplooey now and then. In an effort to save time and handle everything efficiently it can all blow up in our faces and make more work for us. A good example of that is when I ran into my sister in the grocery store after work recently and she was wearing open toed shoes with only one big toe painted red and nothing on the rest of her piggies. Looking down at her feet I joked, "Just one toe polished? Too tired to do the rest?" After simmering for a minute she confessed to a multi-tasking nightmare. She was going through the automated car wash and not being able to stand the fact that she had a whole three minutes with nothing to do but sit still and be patient she decided to paint her toe nails. Now if you're asking yourself right now, "What kind of a person would paint their toe nails while going through a car wash?" that would be my sister. Unfortunately she only got the big toe done when the whole car jerked and the bottle of polish spilled all over the car floor. What a mess – she spent the rest of the time trying to clean the carpet.

Of course I'm guilty myself of trying to do too much in too little time – my sister took one look at the crotch on my pants and asked why it was covered in white splotches. On my way out the door to work that morning I decided to hit the toilet one more time before rushing out of there. As I'm on the bowl staring at my son's toothpaste spit in the sink in front of me I lean over and grab a Clorox wipe and decide to clean it. Yes my house is that small that I can sit on the bowl and clean the sink AND the shower at the same time. This is what being a mother is like – you can't even pee in peace without cleaning or bandaging something. Unfortunately I didn't notice until I got to work much later that I had spilled some of the bleach in the canister onto my pants in the process. So there I was in the grocery store after work trolling for some grub for my brood walking around with a bleached crotch and looking at my sister with one big red toe. Then I looked around at other women dragging kids around the store in about the same shape we were.

Yup, trying to keep all the balls in the air in a juggling act of multi-tasking boot camp you might drop one now and then. We should all band together and start our own circus – the Mom's Circus Club – able to juggle all that life throws at us while balancing on the nose of a platypus.

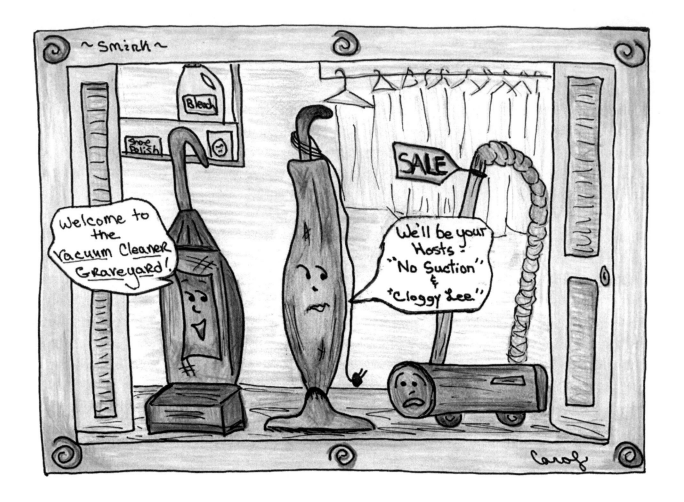

~ DISORGANIZED DOMESTICATION ~

I hope I'm not the only one out there that struggles with the daily grind of trying to keep your house clean and everything running smoothly throughout the week. It's as nerve-wracking as a big exam you suddenly have to cram for. If there were a category on Jeopardy for this it would probably be, "Disorganized Domestication."

I actually don't mind housework so much, but getting the time to do it is the real issue. I have no idea how other people do it. I have one friend whose house is absolutely immaculate and they actually have white carpet. White carpet — the thought of it just blows my mind! The place is spotless — you could probably lick the toilet seat and not catch any germs. Not that I would actually lick a toilet seat….. well, maybe for a million dollars I would.

I start off my week on Sunday with the place all in order, dishes washed, laundry put away, food shopping done, floors mopped and everything organized. By Wednesday the place could be condemned, not one pair of clean underwear anywhere to be found, yogurt has been ground into the sofa, we're out of milk and bread, and there's not a clean cup or spoon in the place. The kids go to school with one blue sock and one black sock and I show up to work looking like 'who did it an ran'. The coffee shop girl will even comment, "Holy smokes, what happened to you?" which really boosts my ego.

By mid-week if someone shows up to my house without calling first it's like some crazed game show dashing throughout the house to shove dirty dishes in the oven, cheerios swept under the rug and spraying Febreeze everywhere to complete the facade of cleanliness. I sweat it out jamming the closet full with the rest of the contents of the house squeezing the door shut hoping it doesn't explode in front of my guests. Of course if it does I'd have to innocently blame it on the kids of course. Kinda like blaming the dog when you have a little gas.

On Monday the kid's lunch boxes contain snacks of healthy fruit, a V-8, and a little smiley note with some stickers and a napkin. By Thursday we've lost the lunch box, I've only been able to find stale crackers at the bottom of the cabinet, a bottle of seltzer, and it's all thrown into a plastic grocery bag. The smiley note has been swapped out with a threatening letter to ban TV for life if they don't shape up and the stickers now have to be scraped off the car door. Napkin? What's a napkin?

My least favorite household chore is the seasonal "changing of the guard" when you have to take out all the spring and summer clothes and put the winter ones away or vice-versa. It's especially tedious doing it for children since they grow out of everything so fast. Doing piles of what goes to the goodwill, what gets passed on to younger relatives, and what goes to the consignment shop is enough to warrant a couple shots of Jack Daniels.

Then there's the job of having to take off all the tags/pins/stickers off the new clothes. Why on earth the manufacturers have to put the tags on with those plastic string thingy attachments is beyond me. (They actually have a word for them but I can't remember it and it's probably something stupid like a "tag harness") I can never find a scissor, so then I have to strain myself pulling them off and the little plastic end piece inevitably falls under the bed where it will sit forever more because there's no way I'm getting my fat butt down under there for a half inch piece of plastic.

The worst is when you're done with the kid's clothes and you have to do yours. It's a slap in the face dealing with the disheartening fact that you've grown out of your clothes due to the winter bulge. The disgust is enough to make you think about dusting off the treadmill for almost a whole five minutes before convincing yourself they've all shrunk in storage somehow and you'll just have to buy new clothes.

All this reminds me of this old lady that won millions in the lottery and when asked what was the first thing she was going to buy with her riches she replied, "I'm gonna git me one them long handled toilet brushes so I don't gotta break my back no more." Some day if I win the lottery I'm going to invest in a self-cleaning house. If they can make a self-cleaning oven I'm sure there's a way they can make a self cleaning house.

"I got a new vacuum cleaner," my mother joyously blurts out over the phone. The woman is clearly addicted to floors you can eat off of. She obsessively cleans her floors and owns about every mop, broom, swiffer, rumba, several various vacuums of sizes and varieties (which is crazy since she has a central vacuum system that works fine) a carpet sweeper (remember those?), and dust busters of all sorts. "It's my thing," she shrugs. "All women have that one *thing* that they are particular about and when they go into another woman's home they always check to see if it's clean… you can tell a lot about a woman by how she keeps her house, ya know." Hmmm… now that's interesting.

I remember my college roommate always saying that her "thing" was the base of the toilet where the knob is. She would always check that when going to other people's homes to see if they had skipped that part and not cleaned it since most people typically would. I always forget the base of the toilet…those knobs are just such a pain the ass.

Got me to thinking if other women do that to – have that one cleaning pet peeve of theirs they set as the high bar standard of suitable cleanliness and if they actually check it out when going to other people's abodes. Maybe my mother knew what she was talking about for a change. I decided to take a little informal poll of some family and friends and see if my mom was right and test her theory.

Over a glass of wine I asked my friend Dawn if she had a cleaning "thing" that she looks for in an effort to judge the character of her hostess. Well that set something off because I got a forty-five minute rant on the importance of cleaning the floor molding - how everyone always forgets that, especially her daughter-in-law, and how can anyone in their right mind not see all the dust caked on there and not take that extra minute to do it, and how everyone does the floor but always forgets the molding and it sickens her to no end. I don't think she paused to inhale once… oh yeah, I hit a nerve… good thing we had wine.

Well apparently dusty molding is a real hot button with other women as well. My cousin Barbara quickly stated, "Over the door molding and the tops of the doors – when I go to somebody's home when they're not looking I run my finger along the top of the door." Hell she better not come over my house then because being four foot nothin' it never occurs to me to do the tops of the doors. Hmm… I don't think I've EVER cleaned the tops of my doors…. Crap… now I'm gonna have to do it because it's gonna make me paranoid that people are coming to my house and judging me by my dusty door tops.

A big ta-do with my Grandmother was the cobwebs in the ceiling corners; drove her nuts and then she'd drive my mother nuts about it. Whenever she'd come over my parent's house she'd be on my mother about the cobwebs along the ceiling. Yet another thing that I never get to. (I'm starting to think I'm a lousy house cleaner now).

The best one by far though was from my friend Sarah. She's is a clean freak germ-a-phobe and the question stumped her into silence – apparently she couldn't pick just "one" cleaning pet peeve. Apparently EVERYTHING is the utmost necessity and must be bleached and scrubbed to the point of sick obsession. How could she possibly pick one "thing" that she looks for in another woman's home that is really important to her that it be clean? The question blew her mind and she obsessed over which one to pick for hours and hours, long after I went home and forgot about it. She called me up at 2am and with crazed exasperation blurted out, "STAIRS! Can't help it – when walking up them you tend to look down at the stairs so you don't trip and can't help but notice the dog hair and dust in the corners of each step. A woman's gotta have clean stairs in my book or she's dead to me."

Well I had to admit my mother's statement had a ring of truth to it. I went over to tell her about my poll results and found my father in the garage putting away the leaf blower on his new shelving unit by the workshop table. I complimented him on the new shelves and how organized he was and he says, "You can tell a lot about a man by how he keeps his garage…."

~ THE 9 MONTH MILE ~

Man, I've seen a whole lotta' pregnant ladies lately. Got me thinking back to both my pregnancies with my daughter and son ….. oh, the living nightmare it all was. I couldn't have been one of those perky Barbie doll types that had a great pregnancy, hardly a weight gain, no nausea, no weird rashes, hormonal surges, or sudden facial hair developing. No, mine was the challenge of a lifetime that should have been an Olympic sport honoring me with a flippin' gold medal when my water broke. The first three months I spent with my head in the toilet pretty much. Why they can come up with a little blue pill to keep a man's penis erect till he's a 104 years old but it's okay for a woman to vomit 24hrs. a day for 90 days without a solution, I'll never know (Poor Viagra – they get blamed for everything).

I had morning sickness, afternoon sickness, midnight sickness, and that 3am sickness in your sleep that you thought you dreamt but unfortunately woke up to realize it was all too real when you find puke on the pillow. I christened every street in my county, a few others, and at least one or two other states. The Sanitation department gave me such dirty looks for months and I had panic attacks thinking the cops were gonna haul me outta' the house in handcuffs. I could see the headlines, "Preggo gets busted for puking on streets; Sanitation Dept Pissed".

Seriously, "Morning Sickness" is no joke. And no matter how many weird home remedies involving eating crackers in bed at 6am, or preggo-lollipops meant as a cure-all, or those messed up acupressure wrist bands that hurt like hell - none of it seemed to work for me. I took everyone's advice from eating oranges to ginger, to "smiling" when I'm nauseous which is supposed to stop the urge. Lord! I thought for sure I'd be dead by the fourth month into what was supposed to be a "special time" of my life where I should look like a glowing angel. My husband had the flu and vomited for 24 hours and all I could say was, "Tough Shit! Try having it for three months, you Wus!" Ahh…mood swings – the other evil you haven't tried before.

Don't get me started on the whole boob issue. I felt like I was gonna tip over being so top heavy. "I mean, seriously, how much milk does the kid need anyways?!" I thought to myself. I could've started my own dairy and hocked it to those funky organic health food places!! Slap a label on a jug that says, "*Carol's Farms* ~ Best Breast Milk on the Planet ~ Now in new Lightweight Containers!"

Oh God, and the pressure to breast-feed because it's so healthy for the baby is so intense from your doctor and family members. I was railroaded into doing it for fear of being seen as a "bad mother", although I'm pretty sure the kids didn't enjoy it so much… being part Italian equates to hairy nipples and the poor things just kept hackin' up hairballs like a cat. Wrecked the hell outta' my boobs too - they hung so low in the aftermath I coulda' tied them into a bow. Years later in a mid-life crisis I burst into a plastic surgeon's off in exasperation and yelled, "Do Something, Dammit, PLEASE!" A week later I walked out of there with brand new 17 year old ta'ta's. Flippin' breast feedin'!

Oh, hell, don't even getting me started on picking out the names. Everyone wants a piece of the pie telling you to name your child after some great Aunt or some Vietnam buddy that saved your Father's life… yadda yadda. Unfortunately those names are always something really horrid like, Bertha, Rocco, Gertrude or Jarvis. I love the people that name their kids after their hometowns or favorite cities like

Dakota, Boston, Cheyenne etc… hmpft… notice ya' don't often see too many kids named "Hoboken" though…

Well, with all those baby books that boast over 35,000 names we couldn't seem to find ONE we agreed upon for the whole nine month mile. I had nightmares thinkin' the kid would be five years old and we'd be callin' it "Hey you". With my son we finally told the Ultra sound technician that she had to help us out and come up with a name… skies the limit… maybe something to show the little guy's Italian heritage… basically laying it on her shoulders to name our child agreeing to go with whatever she came up with. She said, "Lucca" and we agreed. Ironically enough it was my husband's mother's maiden name. We threw in my maiden name as his middle name and he became the boy with three last names.

I admit I was a nervous wreck during my first pregnancy and read every baby book I could get my hands on and watched every "Baby Story" episode on cable watching over a hundred women push kids out of their vaginas for months. I thought for sure I would accidentally kill my kid in the first week of its life. I figured I've killed almost every houseplant I've ever had and my last pet committed suicide. I must have dropped my niece on the floor about eight times in the first six months of her life. I'm surprised she doesn't have brain damage. I was a nanny for a short period of time and I was terrible at it. On my second day I was writing a note to the nursery school teacher saying Jimmy and Sue couldn't make it to playtime because they were hung-over. They got into their father's beer as I was cleaning toothpaste off the TV from the other two hoodlums. Two year old Sue was crying into her sippy cup and all Jimmy could do was hold his head and pathetically whine, "Make her stoooooopppp!!!!" obviously experiencing his first hang over at the tender age of three.

My girlfriend recently had a baby. One day when I was visiting her she was changing the baby's diaper. The baby was a little over a week old and that black belly button nub thing was still there and hadn't fallen off yet. Just as I was thinking "I hope that thing doesn't cut loose with me being here and all" it does. She picks up the naked baby out of the old diaper and the thing pops off like a champagne cork and goes flying across the linoleum. Before I could express any emotion at all, quick as flash, the dog runs over and snaps it up like a doggy treat and one swallow later it was gone forever. All I could do was drop my jaw to the ground and look horrified with shock and disgust and scream loudly, "DID YOU JUST SEE THAT??!!!" "MY, GOD!!" "COULD HE DIE??!!"

Now if this isn't shocking enough to blow your mind my friend goes after the dog and grabs its muzzle and sticks her fingers down it's throat, all the while yelling "Bad Dog! Spit it out!" Jesus, I think this goes a little bit beyond what I think of as "bad dog". Then to be gutsy enough to try to go after it was enough to make me wet myself. I thought she was trying to save the life of the dog, but she wasn't, she actually wanted the thing back to put in her scrapbook. Oy, vey!

I had forgotten about the "Baby's First Year" Scrapbook you get at your baby shower that you're all happy and gung-ho to do in the blissful beginnings of motherhood. You rush to fill it with pictures and notes of their "first bath", "first haircut", "first spoonful of baby food" etc… and fill it with a zillion pictures. By the time you get to the second, third or fourth kid those books aren't filled out and you're lucky if you have one picture of the fourth kid even for identification purposes in case of a kidnappin'. It's always the last one that get's jipped out of a baby book, poor thing.

Yup… that nine month mile is a tough one to endure. By the time the eighth month rolls around you just want to beg the doctor to cut you open and drag the kid out 'cuz you can't take it anymore. You've puked for months, you look like a blob, you can't find ANY position that allows you to sleep, the peeing is out of control and so are the hemorrhoids. All the panicking wondering how bad labor is gonna hurt doesn't seem to bother you so much because at least you know it will be over then. And let me just say, I am no hero – when I went to that hospital the first thing I said was "Get me drugs and lots of 'em – Screw that Lamaze shit" and ordered three rounds of Stadol for my IV like a waiter was taking my selections from the medical menu. Unfortunately the other women down the hall opted to be good mommies and go au 'naturale… Amongst the painful screams, I swear I think I heard one of them say, "You and your @#$% Viagra are the cause of this!!"

~ POTTY TRAINING: THE OTHER EVIL ~

I love animals and children, but they both create a lot of work. I figure it's probably about 75% work with a miniscule 25% return on my investment in the form of pleasure. Here's the problem: anything that requires me to clean up poop makes me an unhappy girl. Dogs/cats/fish/children all require one to participate in cleaning of such. You just can't get away from the stuff.

Trying to potty train my children was like the seventh ring of Dante's Inferno. True hell! Both my children refused to be potty trained. I had visions of them graduating high school in "Depends" adult diapers. No amount of coaxing would do it, but I was driven like Scarlett O'Hara, "As God as my witness, I shall never change another diaper again!" I was determined to save the $4,500 a year I spent in diapers. All the magazine articles on the subject say to reward them with stickers when they go. My daughter was too smart for that.

"Honey, if you just *try* to sit on the potty…just sit on it…then Mommy will give you a Cinderella sticker."

Her response? "Grandma gives me stickers whenever I want, and I don't have to sit on the potty to get them." For boys, they suggest putting cheerios in the bowl and letting them take aim. My son just put his hand in, plucked them out, and ate them. He couldn't understand why I was putting food in the toilet, so then I tried putting in little boats for him, but then he flushed the toilet to see how they'd do in the 'perfect storm'. So after the toilet literally exploded and the plumbing bill cleaned out my account, he cried when I wouldn't let him play with his boat after it sailed the seven seas of the septic system. This was another helpful potty training tip from *Parenting* magazine that failed miserably.

With animals it's worse, because you have to pick up after them, and just saying, "pooper scooper" makes me convulse uncontrollably. Thank God my parents moved out to the country when we were kids so we could just open the back door and let our pets roam the fifteen acres we had. Unfortunately, they wouldn't come back, and we would have to call them for an hour screaming their names like idiots off the back porch, "Bach! Beethoven! Mozart!" The neighbors were really stumped as to why we were nightly screaming the names of dead composers for all the world to hear. So then we had to start walking them on leashes at 6 a.m. each morning, and I can't tell you how many times I missed the school bus because the dog was constipated. Try writing that on a note to the teacher as an excuse for tardiness. "Carol was late to school because the dog couldn't take a dump this morning."

I suppose eventually the tables will turn though. When I'm ninety-three and in a wheelchair wearing "Depends," I'll simply smirk and tell my daughter, "Touché".

~ THE APRON STRINGS OF MOTHERHOOD ~

Ahh… the loving apron strings of Motherhood…. One minute they're comforting and the next they're the ties that will bind and choke you to death. The Mother-Daughter relationship is a strange and wonderful thing that has kept the therapists employed down through the ages. I'm pretty sure Cleopatra and her mother had issues as well.

"Cleo, what is with all that blue stuff on your eyes?"

"It's called 'make-up,' mother and I just invented it to go along with my toga for cruising down the Nile, duhhhhhh."

"Keep it up, missy, and you'll be staying home cleaning out the snake cages this weekend."

My own mother knew she was going to get a run for her money when she came to pick me up from the first day of kindergarten. As she was chatting with all the other neighborhood 1950's ladies, they walked into the room for an unusual scene. All the little girls were playing "house" in the kitchen area while all the little boys were wide eyed and sucking their thumbs watching little old me working up a sweat in my pink sundress beating the hell out of the punching bag. "Oh, is that *your* darling little angel?" the ladies asked my mother with a raised brow. She knew then I was gonna be trouble.

By second grade, I came home from school wearing a trench coat and nothing but my duckie Underroos underneath. "Practicing for a career as a flasher?" she said. "I lost my dress," I grumbled. Stunned, she wondered aloud how the hell I could lose the clothes off my back. I actually was doing a few different skits in the school variety show and for one number I had to wear my tu-tu (what a great word — tu-tu — I just love saying it) and when I went to change back to my dress, it was gone. The school bus was leaving and the teacher didn't know what to do so she just threw my trench coat on and shoved me on the bus. Of course I was made fun of all the way home since my brother wound up with my dress somehow and waved it around like a flag letting everyone know I was stripped down to my skivvies. Looking back, I can now undeniably say I have always found myself in a bit of pickle.

It didn't get any better through my school years. I got in trouble in fourth grade for knocking the teeth out of two different boys. The dental bills were enormous, and I had to fork over my allowance for what I justified as 'defending my honor'. By middle school, my mother lectured me about jumping off a bridge like everyone else after I got caught smoking my first cigarette at the church dance. In high school, the lecture changed to getting the cow and the milk for free after getting my first kiss behind the school gym. In college, I was cautioned about cults, booze, and STD's. By the time my thirties hit, she was complaining that I needed to settle down and give her some grandchildren. Now that I have an ex-husband and my children are little terrors these days, she sighs with disappointment, "This is not the life I wanted for you."

What is it about this love-hate struggle we have with our mothers and eventually our daughters? We try to inspire and encourage one another without being too overly critical, but both parties always seem to be frustrated in the end. We laugh with each other until we cry, scream at each other until someone gets slapped, shop 'til we drop, and console each other in the most tragic of circumstances like no other person can. Your mother is the one person that will take you in at 4 a.m. no questions asked - just a hug. No matter how old you get, a warm bed, your hair stroked, a hot cup of cocoa, and your mother's shoulder to cry on always seem to do the trick when life gets you down. This will be the same mother you will abuse heavily, screaming that you're never going to talk to her again bringing up everything she did wrong in your childhood. How we reward our mothers for their love.

I think about all this when I see my own little girl dressed up in Wizard of Oz ruby slippers, a yellow-polka dot skirt, purple feather boa, and a princess crown, and I wonder what I have in store over the next couple of decades. When she gets angry and yells, "Bad Mommy" to me and then the next minute sucks her thumb and curls up on my lap, I wonder how we'll get through it all. Will I be saying, 20 years from now, "This is not the life I wanted for you." Sigh… I need to go have a chat over coffee with my mother.

~ "I'D DO ANYTHING FOR LOVE BUT I WON'T SEW THAT…" ~

Being all cooped up in the house weathering storms and a ton of rain as March comes in like a lion gives one the opportunity to catch up on some projects that have been piling up. You get the chance to catch up on a hobby you've been wanting to pick up again or start that new book you've been wanting to read. With me I finally got around to pulling out the sewing box because I wanted to sew the button back on my jacket — people were beginning to throw coins at me on the street like I was a pauper for cryin' out loud. Then I started to think about the whole pile of clothes in the laundry basket in the corner for the last six months needing some sort or sewing repair. So the piper came a callin' with put-off sewing as that rainy day ticket came due and I grudgingly decided to tackle it.

Unfortunately when other members of the family see you sewing something everyone wants in on the action. Suddenly there's a line out the door like you just opened up a tailor shop. "Mommy, can you put the stuffing back into Bridget and sew her legs back on?" "Honey, can you take up this pair of pants for me… and this one too…oh wait…just one more….pretty please?" "The zipper broke on my jacket and grandma said if you were a good mother you would have fixed it by now." "Honey, can you sew the side pocket of my jacket?" Even the little guy gets in on it: "Mommy, can you sew Doggie's eye back on?" Before long I threw the sewing box aside and went straight for the big guns — the Sewing Machine. I ripped that baby out and became "Xena, Queen of the Kenmore." I had to sew a hole in a glove, a rip in a favorite pair of Scooby Doo socks that couldn't be parted with, a patch job on the quilt I've been meaning to get to, and hemmed about ten pairs of pants for various family members.

My sister heard from my mother who heard from my sister-in-law that I had pulled out the sewing machine and quicker than you can say "twitter" she was at my door with a stack of "skirts, shirts and pants, oh my!" You see everyone in my family is a hobbit — you could lay a board across our heads and it would be perfectly level at five feet. Everyone needs everything taken up and it gets pricey, so when a sewing machine gets pulled out the word gets out quick. Just once it would be nice to buy a shirt I didn't have to take the sleeves up on or a pair of pants that didn't need to be taken up at the knee just so we could walk in them. The amount of fabric I gotta cut off family clothing could be used to make a quilt that would cover the whole flippin' state.

So after performing major surgery on Bridget for which she came out of it not only new and improved but with a new pair of hair ribbons, and sewing just about everything in the house from the curtains to the tassels on the couch pillows (went a little needle happy) and dozens upon dozens of pants, etc. I came to a halt as I came to the bottom of the sewing basket at the one thing I absolutely refused to sew. There it was at the bottom of the mountain of stuff I sewed that day … begging for its frayed end to be repaired …. *A pink tie*. I shuddered like I was singing Meatloaf's "I'd do anything for love…. but I won't do that!" I simply *abhor* the pink tie!

Every man that wears one from anchorman to sports coach suddenly loses my respect when they venture into that most unnatural of territories. I was disappointed one night as I sat and counted how many men were wearing pink ties from Jeopardy's Alex Trebec and NBC reporter Brian Williams to sports commentators Mike Ditka and Terry Bradshaw. I was just so disgusted to count about 35 men in the public eye wearing various shades of fuchsia pink, pastel pink, rose colored polka dots, coral shaded stripes, and pink cotton candy paisley.

Here's the thing: men should never wear pink. Plain and simple it's a female color and they can't pull it off! *Hell no!* Makes me really want to barf. It's just all wrong. It's like buying a sweater for a fish and we're not in any Dr. Seuss reality here. It's just not attractive. Taking the soft feminine warm tones of "pink" and combining it with the ultimate male symbol that wreaks of masculinity, the "tie", and you get the odd red headed step-child of *"the pink tie"*. It's an anomaly in the system that must be destroyed.

For cryin' out loud, there's very little women can claim as their own in this world and if there is one thing, hands down, that we should be able to stake a victory flag on, it should be the color pink! Really! It's a sad attempt to once again have something they can't have and want it "just because."

So I stared down at that sewing basket and thought about what to do with this lovely pink tie with sweetheart roses on it in front of me… Hmmm….I wondered.

A couple hours later my honey was watching my daughter play with her Barbie that had a lovely knew pink evening gown on it. He says to me, "Boy that dress looks a little like my favorite pink tie... you know… the one with the roses on it… can't seem to find it… have you seen it?" I smirk and mumble, "I don't know what 'yer talkin' about," as I shove the still smokin' Kenmore back into the closet for another rainy day...

~ A TREASURED TOY ~

I was watching that "Toy Story" movie for the zillionth time the other night with my kids. That popular film about a child's special toys, Woody and Buzz Lightyear, got me thinkin' about your typical child's treasured "friend" that they rely each night to cuddle with in bed, drag everywhere, and consider part of the family.

Who could forget the beloved "Mrs. Beazley" that Buffy from "A Family Affair" TV show dearly coveted in the 70s? Her blue dress with white polka dots and thick rimmed glasses are recognizable even to this day. My grandmother fondly remembers a porcelain doll with a cracked head she got as a Christmas present one year during the depression. Even though a doll with a cracked head out of the trash was all she got, it was dearly treasured and we're always reminded of how lucky we are. "We had nothin' during the depression and we were damn glad to have that," she growls from time to time. My mother loved the ever-popular Raggedy Ann & Andy dolls, and carried them until they were truly "rags" held together by more thread than fabric. Then there was that whole era of Cabbage Patch dolls that frenzied parents went crazy for at Christmas, trying to get one for their kids before they sold out.

In our family my daughter has a stuffed animal that's either a cheetah or jaguar, we can never tell. She named it "Cleopatra" and she is rarely without it. Cleopatra is getting a bit worn, has been on many travels, slept on every night, and has had to be Fed-Ex'd overnight when she was accidentally left behind at a relative's in Connecticut. Last year she had to have her butt sewn up — God only knows how that happened but suddenly we noticed a small little cheetah or jaguar that looked similar to Cleopatra amongst the hoard of stuffed animals. My daughter is convinced it's Cleopatra's baby that she had in the middle of the night somehow. Nice to know I sewed up an episiotomy on the old gal. Of course I suspiciously eyed the rest of the stuffed animals on the bed with a raised brow, sneering, "All right, which one of you Casanova's is the father?" Nobody owned up and Cleo wasn't talkin'. So we named our new addition "Patches" but mostly we just called her "Cleo's baby".

Now although I am not a fan of stuffed animals or blankies I did have one that I took a liking to as a child. I found him the other day while digging through an old box of childhood memorabilia. After digging a little bit, there he was …. a bit tattered and dusty but the same as I remembered…. a stuffed clown with a pink nose named "Willy". Well, actually his official name was "Willy 2" because both my sister and I received the same stuffed clown for Christmas one year and she came up with the name Willy and I honestly thought that was the best name for the little guy so hers was named "Willy" and mine was "Willy 2". He looked a little forlorn being in the box for a decade and secretly pouted for a day I'm sure. He got over it pretty quickly though because the next morning I caught him and Cleopatra in bed together. "Aha!" I exclaimed at them both, "Now in addition to Patches we're bound to have another mouth to stuff in nine months." I swore Willy smirked at me.

~ THE SIBLING RIVALRY DANCE ~

So I was talking to my sister the other day and she was commenting about how the sibling rivalry is already starting between her new baby and her kindergartener. Apparently the baby is teething all over everything and somehow gnawed and/or slobbered the corner of my niece's favorite Strawberry Shortcake book. Stomping her little feet and scowling her brow, she pouted that the baby wasn't being fair and those were her toys.

I laughed and shook my head, "Oh, you have no idea how bad it's gonna get… just wait till they're out of car seats and old enough to kick and punch each other in the back seat," I told her. Right now I'm in the "yelling phase" which is a recent addition to the everyday splattering of playing Referee. It's like a nice seasoning to the boring daily complaints of "Mom! He took my stuff" followed by, "You love her more than me!" and of course my all time favorite, "It's not fair." Hell, I'd be cringing on what it's gonna be like in the teen years, if I wasn't so focused on just trying to keep them alive one more day with as little bloodshed as possible….I figured my best bet was to start putting all my spare change in a wine bottle to save up for all the therapy they're gonna need later. Emptying the wine bottles to store the change in will be MY therapy.

Why is it that it's always World War III in the back seat of the car whenever you're trying to drive somewhere? It's an endless onslaught of 'who started it first' and 'who hit who first' and then there's the "I hate you, poopy face" and "Well, I hate you more, butt brain" which eventually leads to somebody getting hit in the head and a drink spilled all over one of them. I wonder what the research is on how many car accidents happen each year due to the stress caused by our young duking it out in the backseat like its Rocky 12. How many times have we heard our parents and now ourselves yell, "Knock it off back there, so help me God, or I'm pulling this car over!" I'm pretty sure that one goes back to 'Little House on the Prairie' days with Pa Ingalls angrily yelling at Laura and Albert to keep it down in the back of the covered wagon or he was gonna ram the horse up a tree.

One thing for sure is when you become a parent you finally understand your own parents and the struggles they went through with you because now you're dealing with the same crap. God only knows the sibling rivalry between me and my three siblings was legendary and I have no idea how we didn't drive my mother to drink. We always seemed to be at each other's throats and getting into mischief until my mother couldn't stand it anymore and would yell to go outside and find something to do.

Unfortunately going outside in the back woods only gave us more trouble to get into and it usually involved power tools, machinery and other elements of destruction that could have easily killed a brother or two. Good lord if my mother only knew how many times we threw rocks at each other in the backyard like we were having a snowball fight, or had an occasional "chase your brother with an ax because he hit you with a rock" game, or enjoyed the always entertaining past time of catching frogs and snakes to fling at one of your brood when they least suspected it… like when they were on the toilet and forgot to lock the door. Double daring a sibling to eat poison berries, grab honey from a swarming hive, roll around in poison ivy, or provoke the bull next door (which usually resulted in a sibling getting chased in a stampede across a cow pie field) was considered common place among my kin. Hmmm...... looking back on my childhood perhaps my kids aren't as intolerable as I thought.

So I try to remember this when they're goin' at it about 'whose turn is it to pick out the next TV show' and how 'he won't give the remote back' and then they're brawling on the carpet and upsetting the dog. In frustration I grab them both by their ears to separate them and demand, "What do you have to say for yourselves?!" Without missing a beat, my little 6 year old son, panting with deep frustration sneers, "I miss the good ol' days when I was a baby."

~ EVEN THE TOOTH FAIRY IS ON UNEMPLOYMENT ~

Get this crap: the economy is so tough that it has taken a bite out of what kids get for losing teeth. A survey by Visa says that the recession has caused a drop in the average amount the Tooth Fairy pays for a tooth, from $3 to $2.60.

Clearly this is a prime expenditure to cut back on when you're feeling strapped. "Hmmm… should we try to cut down on the amount of beer we suck down in a week or screw the kid out of his tooth fairy money, Sweetheart, whadaya think?"

Visa must be bored or have money to burn if they're actually doing stupid surveys like this. Can you flippin' believe they even broke it up by geographical area? Apparently the West isn't too bad – the tooth fairies there coughed up an average of a dime more this year as compared to the East Coast where it dropped over a buck eighty. Apparently getting money out of the Jersey Tooth Fairy is like pulling teeth. She'll be forced to do some fairy-godmothering on the side just to make ends meet. The Southern Tooth Fairy works the hardest with all the toothless red neck wonders down there. She's so broke she leaves them a beat up couch on their front lawn and a coupon for grits. The one up North in Canada shells out French coins with a note that says, "Brush your teeth more, ya little hoser!"

"So what's the going rate on teeth these days?" my Third grader asked me yesterday. When prompted why she needed to know she explained that she's getting ripped off because her cousin got $5 and she only got a buck. I had to explain that the tooth fairy that works in Westchester has a lot more money to go around then the one up here. Not sure if she bought it. I got a dirty look and the real estate pages handed to me. According to one Boston Website the kids were getting up to $10 per tooth there – good thing she didn't see that or we'd be developing horrible accents right now.

Some kids say they plan on saving their tooth fairy money for something special – like a video game or candy; both of which rot your remaining teeth and brains. When I was a kid I got a quarter which was the exact amount for "fines" in my house for yelling. You yell at a sibling you put a quarter in the bad behavior jar. So that's where all my tooth fairy money came from.

A co-worker's child just had his first tooth come out while riding on the school bus. Not thinking anything of it the little guy just threw it out. Clearly he didn't know this was a prime money-making opportunity. If this happens with other children the poor tooth fairy will be on the unemployment line... although I do hear that there's a support group for Unicorns, the Easter Bunny, Santa, and Sasquatch that maybe she can get in on for some coping skills.

My little guy just turned 6 years old and still hasn't had any teeth fall out yet. He's getting frustrated seeing his friends lose theirs and getting rewarded for it with cold hard cash so he's seeking alternatives. He has a list of ideas such as knocking a few out himself with his plastic toy hammer from his tool kit, stealing his great grandmother's dentures, knocking off a dentist's office, or making a deal for some on the kindergarten black market. What a racket. Unfortunately when he finally does have some teeth to cough up for the "under-the-pillow-transference-of-goods-for-cash" routine, she might be giving him an "IOU"!

~ "I'M CUCKOO FOR COCO PUFFS!" ~

A recent discussion on my health nut brother's blog says that he's into a new kind of cereal. *Kashi* rocks and sticks or something — and it got me thinking about how generally most people enjoy a good bowl of cereal. Any combination of sugar, crunch, grain, fruit, nutty, yummy confection variety that could be concocted has been the staple of the American population since the beginning of time. *Captain Crunch, Cheerios, Lucky Charms, Grape Nuts, Frosted Flakes* — just gotta love 'em.

I'm pretty positive Adam sat around dunking his donuts in some milk and eventually threw it in a bowl and dumped the milk on top to make it easier and then Eve had that great idea of putting a slice of banana on it and bam — cereal was invented.

Cereal is amazing any time of the day and fills the void with hardly any prep work. Any avoidance of cooking when you're flat out starving and don't have time is a good time for cereal. Kids driving you nuts when you're in the middle of something? "Go eat a bowl of cereal — that should hold you till dinner." My motto is if it's cheap, tasty and easy, we buy buckets of it. Middle of the night and you can't sleep? Cereal to the rescue.

The dinner got burned and nobody can stomach it? Rip out those colorful boxes of Tony the Tiger, dancing leprechauns, cuckoo birds, Captain Crunch, along with a rabbit that refuses to believe that Trix are for kids and Count Chocula of course! They all boast of magical toy surprises inside and enough vitamins, minerals and fiber to fuel a racehorse. The only thing that could suck about that is if the stores are closed and you're out of milk.

Any type of bowl will do. On occasion my friend has come home after a night on the town to a sink full of dishes and actually resorted to using the glass measuring cup as her bowl. I myself have had to eat cereal out of a recycled margarine tub I consider as my finest Tupperware containers.

If you're a real aficionado of cereal you can actually get a personalized cereal bowl like 'Carol's Cereal Bowl' made up. There's a company on the Internet that is just over-run at Christmas with orders. I know because I bought one and had to wait two months for it. In an era of getting things zapped in front of us like the blink of 'I dream of Jeannie's' eyes, two months is like the pony express — but with maybe a goat instead of a horse.

Everyone in the family has their favorites of course. My daughter sticks straight to plain Cheerios and has no interest in anything else. I made the mistake of trying to switch it up one week and get the Honey Nut Cheerios which she didn't like apparently and it sits there. There's always one box of something you got that nobody liked so it just sits in the cabinet, probably stale by now since it's been months, but nobody wants to throw it out in the event of a food shortage and your forced to eat it or somebody gets hungry enough and lowers their taste bud standards.

My son refuses to eat at all. The kid just exists on air and I've spent thousands at the Children's Hospital's "Feeding Team" playing "kiss the apple game" for two years trying to get this kid to eat something other than peanut butter. Then someone told him the other day that Fruit Loops makes your poop turn green. He thought that would be cool and now he eats Fruit Loops. Other strange cereal habits of my family include one member that puts maple syrup on their Corn Pops, and another that likes Rice Crispies with Diet Coke instead of milk. I just don't see it myself but to each his own I suppose.

I hate how you get a favorite kind of cereal and then they discontinue it. It's so frustrating! In my teens I loved a cereal called C.W. Post which is similar to low fat granola currently on the shelves, but just not quite the same. It went well sprinkled on top of my apple-cinnamon flavored *Cream of Wheat* hot cereal. Then one day "poof" it was gone off the shelves. I ate this daily for four years straight without missing a day and then suddenly it's just ripped from my daily morning routine and I'm forced to find a substitute? I had no choice in the matter - why didn't they call and let me know so I could stock up on it in a private underground bunker and ration it out to myself for the next few decades? I was really ticked off for not being consulted. I swear my digestive system wasn't happy about it for months.

Then, like a slap in the face, following suit was *Cream of Wheat*. Out of nowhere every store in the tri-state area stopped carrying the apple cinnamon flavor — which is the only one I liked! Believe me - I've gone to enormous lengths to try to get it re-supplied to the public to no avail - no matter how many letters I wrote. All the grocery stores claim if you fill out a form at the courtesy desk for a particular product they will do their best to stock it. Liars! All of them. I've filled out a request for apple cinnamon flavored *Cream of Wheat* in every major chain in a 50-mile radius and I haven't seen a box of it yet.

A friend of mine used to love Quisp cereal in the 70's with the little alien on the front of the box and longs for its chocolatey-chip goodness still. There's actually several websites out there that pay tribute to all the discontinued favorite cereals through history. When Star Wars was popular there was C3PO cereal, which is probably a major collectible now I bet.

Wheaties made every athlete super famous and who could forget the ever popular, Ghostbuster's cereal of the 1990's? When I lived in Buffalo I used to love to eat Flutey Flakes named after the Buffalo Bills Quarterback, Doug Flutie. (Ugh, I'd kill for a box now.) Even Mr. T had his own cereal — "I pity the fool that doesn't eat my cereal!"

We should revolt and have a cereal revolution marching a parade of cereal boxes down Main Street to city hall and demand our favorites be resurrected from the grave. Maybe we can get Mary Poppins to lead the march by sitting on a float made entirely of pastel colored mini-marshmallows while singing, "A spoonful of sugar makes the cereal go down…"

~ HER COOKING COULD KILL A HORSE! ~

I like to think of myself as a bit of a gourmet cook. Chicken Marsala, Sweet potato encrusted Salmon, Beef Wellington — you name it, I can cook it. The fact that no-one eats my food is, I'm sure, chalked up to them being picky eaters. It can't possibly be "me" I reason with myself. The fact that my children eat nothing but peanut butter and jelly sandwiches and turn their nose up at even the toast I make, can't possibly be my fault.

Perhaps it's hereditary, ya' think?! My mother tries like hell but was a little lacking in the domestic area while I was being raised. Opening all the doors and waving the dish towel in front of a blaring smoke alarm was a nightly occurrence. To put it bluntly the woman could burn jello. I have a cast iron stomach from all the tar-like substances I've been fed as a child. You need roughage? Come over my parent's house and you'll be pickin' up your colon off the linoleum — and that's just breakfast. My taste buds have been permanently scarred — maybe that's why nobody will eat my food. It probably tastes like road kill and I'm thinking its filet mignon.

For years I actually thought that mashed potatoes came from a man named Hungry Jack and didn't discover until college that people actually boiled real potatoes and then mashed them up. No wonder Jack was always hungry eating that crap. Spaghetti sauce? More like red colored water over remnants of over-cooked pasta mush. My mother would take tomatoes, put them in the blender, and then just pour the concoction over the noodles with not a hint of any spices. It was a plate of red colored water at the bottom of soggy pasta — nothing stuck to the pasta. A V-8 thrown on there would have had more staying power.

Each year for the holidays I'd look forward to a great tasting turkey only to suffer through a bird so dry there was no amount of gravy that was gonna help it down. Just thinking about it makes me gag thinking I have a bone stuck in my throat. The worst is if it was undercooked — we'd all be killing each other for rights to the toilet. Thank God they finally came up with that little knob in the turkey that goes "boop" when it's done — I like to think that at least I've got a "boop" of a chance at surviving the salmonella now.

Every year I try to create my own dish to enter into the Betty Crocker Cook-off for their million dollar prize. I eagerly wait each spring to watch the televised live finale on the cooking network. One housewife came up with the idea of taking a package of French Toast Sticks, cut them up, added spices to it to make stuffing and then put the little package of maple syrup it came with over some chicken and baked it. Can you flippin' believe she won a million dollars for that? That's just cuckoo bananas right there. So I came up with what I thought was a great casserole of turkey meat, vegetables, egg noodles, a special sauce, and topped with bread crumbs that I was sure would be in the top ten at least. I served it to my family and all my brother could say was, "It tastes like a turkey pot pie," which I considered an insult. No offense, Swanson, but really! A turkey pot pie?! I spent hours coming up with just the right balance of ingredients that Betty Crocker herself would go ga-ga over, for heaven's sake!

I do like to be adventurous at times. I've cooked cow tongue, snake meat, ostrich, alligator, rabbit, and shark. Sad to say only the alligator and ostrich came out okay. The shark tasted like rubber, the cow tongue tasted like a really bad French kiss, and the rest would only be tasty to contestants on "Survivor" that are half starved and would eat your eyeball if given the chance. Hey, maybe that would be a good career move — become a chef cooking platypus for the Survivor show. I'd have a captured audience that would actually eat and enjoy the slop I shove in front of them out of sheer starvation. In that case my kids would be a shoe in to win at that show. The next time they turn their nose up at my entree I'll simply tell them they're in training for Survivor.

~ "YOU GAVE THE HOMELESS, HEARTBURN?" ~

You ever hear the phrase, "No good deed goes unpunished?" Well that could apply to my love of cooking and everyone else's non-love of my cooking. You cook meals for your family with good intentions and then when they turn their nose up at your concoction after slaving over a hot stove it's like a slap in the face. Henceforth that phrase of my good deed getting punished got stuck in my head. Although I do remember a few years back when my cooking created a bit of a catastrophe that I probably deserve to be punished for.

I had just moved to the state of Connecticut and not knowing anyone I thought I'd get involved with the local church women's group. They were all preparing a dish that we could bring to the local homeless shelter to serve to them. I was assigned that typical dish of "green bean casserole" with the Campbell's mushroom soup and French fried onions that just about everyone on the planet has made for Thanksgiving. Well, I had to multiply it by a kajillion amount because we had to make this big huge tin pan of the stuff to feed a couple hundred people. To say I'm not good at math is an understatement and to figure out how much pepper I needed multiplying 1/8th of a teaspoon into vats of green beans proved more than I was capable of apparently.

I stood next to a woman that made the sliced potatoes with melted cheddar cheese. Everyone seemed to like her dish. I shelled out my green beans but after awhile I noticed some of the ragged whino's grabbing their chests in agony and mumbling something about pepper. Then Miss Potato next to me snottily pointed out that they were throwing their plates away with everything eaten but my green beans. So we both tasted the green beans and realized they had way too much pepper in them and heartburn was the result. "Great, you just gave the homeless, heartburn, Carol. They'll be in their little cardboard boxes in the alley tonight cursing you out in agony. I wonder if you can go to hell for that." Needless to say we didn't "click".

Being a trooper I tried again the next month but this time they put me on potato patrol and since it was just slicing potatoes and some onions and covering them with shredded cheddar cheese I figured I couldn't screw that one up.

Nope, I was wrong. I didn't read the recipe right and didn't bake them nearly as long as they should have been. So there I was spooning out my potatoes next to snotty lady who got re-assigned the green bean casserole since I couldn't seem to handle fractions. Once again she was so polite to point out that everyone was throwing away plates with all the potatoes uneaten. Damn, it's a sad day when even bums won't eat your cooking. So we tried my lovely dish and all the potatoes were crunchy raw, the onions too, and the cheese was barely melted. How the hell do I know how long real potatoes cook for – remember my mother only made mashed potatoes from a box growing up. So, it was awful to say the least.

I wasn't asked back by those church ladies again. I had heard that they had gotten complaints from some of the homeless about my culinary expertise. Can you believe that? So I'm sure I'm gonna get that segment of my life played back to me in heaven like a bad reality show video tape…God pointing out the parts that I didn't do so good on. "Hmm… looks like you tried to poison the less fortunate of my flock back in the 90s there, Carol, --- what do you have to say for yourself?" "Poison? Oh, c'mon – it's not like I gave them salmonella for God's sake."

Yeah, I don't stand a chance. If no good deed goes unpunished I imagine mine will be to spend eternity watching bums eat banquets of food while I'm only allowed to eat stale crackers.

~ "SCOOBY DOOBY DOO, WHERE ARE YOU?" ~

We love and cherish our televisions, don't we? Yet we often take modern television for granted whining, "There's nothin' on...," endlessly flipping through hundreds of channels. There's always one night of the week where none of your regular shows are on and you get a cramp in your thumb hitting the "page down" button. You've even gone through what you saved on the DVR but you're just not in the mood for half the stuff you taped. That show from 3 months ago about that castle tour of Ireland is still sitting there but you don't want to delete it in the event you get tanked one night... start seeing leprechauns ... remember the show... and simply MUST watch it. The older generations probably laugh at us. "You kids are all spoiled - I remember back when television wasn't even invented yet and we had to sit around and play charades every weekend – try doing *that* for 30 years."

I tell my own kids about how we constantly got "interference" from other shows and they thought that meant the TV had a virus and the cable company just needed to "re-boot". "We didn't have cable back then – we had this big metal antennae thingy' on the roof." "NO CABLE???!!!" After that I tried telling them that TV actually closed down at night and went off the air and the channels just showed colored vertical lines with a loud "EEEEEEEEEEEE" sound. That just was too much for them to handle -- they went pale as a sheet like I was telling them a terrifying tale around the campfire.

TV has come a long way since the days of "I love Lucy", "Gilligan's Island", and "Hee-Haw". Reality shows have almost made the sitcom extinct. We've gone from "Candid Camera" to "America's Funniest Home Videos". Singing shows like "The Partidge Family" and "Donny and Marie" have morphed into a reality show called "American Idol". Game shows have evolved from the "Gong Show" and "Family Feud" to "Cash Cab" and "Repo Games". Can you believe they actually made a game show out of answering trivia questions to avoid getting your car repossessed?

I started flipping through the channels in pursuit of something decent to mention about modern television. I watched a show called, "Monster Hogs" about crazed gigantic hogs eating up half the south. If you're reading this in Georgia and your toy poodle, "Pinkie Pie" is missing you might want to catch their latest episode. After watching National Geographic for a while I'm convinced Atlantis is still out there. I got a hankering for cupcakes after watching the Cake Boss make a 5-foot cake that looked like Han Solo's Millennium Falcon. Almost immediately I knew to steer clear of a woman named, "Snookie" for fear of catching a venereal disease just watching her show. On the other hand, that "Joe" from "Blues Clues" ain't half bad. Suze Ormon made me want to run out and get an IRA in a mad panic. The "Biggest Loser" had me feeling guilty for eating a half dozen cupcakes after the "Cake Boss" show. Lastly I watched a show on how these 16-year-old conjoined twins were getting their drivers license with one steering and one working the pedals. Andy Rooney would have commented, "I couldn't help but ponder which one of them would get the speeding ticket when they got pulled over."

Well, you can't talk about TV as the most important device and not mention the remote control as its master. You are ruler of your domain when you control the remote. If you misplace the remote for even one day it's like terrorist torture and you rip the house apart looking for it like it was a gold nugget. Nothing frustrates you more than not having your remote. Just ask my first ex-husband - when I found out he was cheatin' with my best friend I didn't get mad... I simply packed a bag and left... but before I did, I turned back, picked up the remotes for the TV, DVR and Stereo then smirked as I threw them in the dumpster down the street.

~ STUPID LAUNDRY OR
LAUNDRY STUPID ~

Like our ever-lovin' tax season there's one other constant in life that everyone has to put up with: the hell that is known as "doing the laundry". We all have to deal with it at some point unless you prefer to be locked up for runnin' around in your birthday suit, are loaded and just wear clothes once and then throw them out, or you have people stealing your dirty clothes from your home each week.

I'm what I would affectionately label "Laundry Stupid". My ex would vouch for that since he had every right to ban me from the laundry room after breaking three brand new washers over three years. That's a heck of an average - breaking one washer per year – guess that would get on anyone's nerves I suppose.

By the time we went for machine number four we decided to buy the best damn washing machine known to man that even I couldn't break. The nice man at Sears said it's a ka-jillion dollars but "you can fit twenty towels in it", which instantly sold me. I was so happy, but when we got home my ex said he was taking over doing the laundry and I wasn't allowed to touch it. Hell – what woman wouldn't want to hear that?! If I knew I'd get out of doing laundry every week, I would have broken them sooner! Woo Hoo!

I suppose I should rewind for a minute here and convey my whole twisted relationship with dirty laundry from the beginning. When I was thirteen my mother entrusted me to do the family laundry one day. She had just bought my brothers and father several new pairs of jeans and told me to take the tags off and throw them in the washer with some detergent and turn the knob like she showed me. I was so proud to be honored with such a big girl responsibility and wanted to go a really good job. The only problem was that I couldn't find any of the usual powered detergent around so I used the only other product she used to clean the clothes. Since I wanted to make a doubly good impression and get them extra super-duper clean, I put the whole container in – the whole thing. This turned out to be a mistake.

When the clothes were done in the washer my mother told me to go downstairs and put them in the dryer. I was a little shocked when I took them out of the washer noticing they came out not looking at all like how they went in. "Wow, this bleach stuff got them a little bit more clean than I had wanted them to be," I thought. I reasoned that after I put them into the dryer they would somehow magically turn back to their original blue jean color minus the white splotches all over them. When they didn't, I dragged them up in the laundry basket flippantly saying, "Mom, the washing machine's broken".

It was at that moment, when I blamed the washing machine and it's side-kick the "dryer", that all the machines everywhere joined together to declare war against me. It was a path of destruction leading to pink "whites", bleached "colors", shredded towels, overflowing bubbles, missing knobs, jammed doors that won't shut, clothes catching fire, zapped circuit board panels, and articles of clothing no-one owned just magically appearing.

I swear no matter how many times I've checked and re-checked putting the whites into a load, it inevitably will come out all pink because a very small red sock will have somehow hid behind a pair of granny panties just to sabotage my load like a filthy spy. Oh – I also don't buy into the belief that if it's too overloaded the clothes won't get clean – that's ridiculous – if there's water and soap they'll get clean. So I make sure every smidgen of that machine is filled to the point of explosion. I don't even "separate" – don't have time for that – just throw a week's worth of laundry in one load whether it's jeans or towels. My sole objective is to get it done and off my mind as quickly as possible. I scoff at products like Woolite for "gentle cleaning" – Ha! Give me the stuff that can clean a car engine and that's my brand, baby! I got kids and that means major stains.

Since my landlord won't spring for a washer/dryer I do all my laundry these days at my parent's house like I did when I was in college. Lord, ya' take two steps forward and one step back in life… middle-aged and my mother's still yelling, "You only come over here to do laundry." So she gets a little irritable when I'm dragging in enough clothes to cover a fleet of naked orphans. "If you break this washer, Carol Ann, we'll ALL be going to the Laundromat!" Now THAT'S a huge threat to me.

Laundromats are mysterious places that always seem to find their way into every chainsaw horror flick out there. Spooky people come out to do their laundry at midnight at the 24 hour ones, and they're a little frightening to say the least. Any minute you're expecting fangs to come out and suddenly you're starring in your own vampire zombie flick.

Basically, me and laundry have been feuding about as long as Snow Meiser and his brother Heat Meiser, and the tales I could tell would leave you in the fetal position, wide-eyed and whispering, "the horror… the horror". Just know that when you see me in public and I'm all wrinkled and wearing bleached jeans with pink socks, I'm not making a fashion statement but rather lost that week's battle with the machines.

~ THE TAMING OF THE UNDERWEAR DRAWER ~

Ever notice during the holidays you get a ton of socks and underwear? That time of year is a good benchmark for checking on the supply of major undergarment necessities. Kinda like the changing of the guard, or how we check our smoke detector batteries at day light savings time each year. No wonder Hanes goes cuckoo bananas with a ton of advertising. So we all get new skivvies but the only problem is that we neglect to throw out the old ones and the underwear drawer starts to get really overstuffed till you can barely close it.

`For gals it's basically a combination of reasons why you don't wear all the stuff in there and it's stuffed to capacity. Some are for specific events only – like your Fredericks of Hollywood thong for a night of la amour (yeah that's right you heard me, Victoria, your Secret is that you're getting' old and boring), and then you have the grandma panties for when Mother Nature bangs down your draw, your man's boxers for when you just want to hang around the house and not shower for two days, and then your basic Monday – Friday no frill basics.

For the guys, you typically overload your drawer with a combination of gag valentine's day g-strings your woman got you one year, the tighty whitey work horse that you should have given up when you were twelve (ugliest creation on the face of the planet, the owner of Fruit of the Loom needs a belt in the mouth for that mess of an undergarment), the worn out pebbled boxers with the hole in the crotch you just LOOOOVE to wear around the house on the weekend that makes your wife pissed, "When the hell are you going to throw those out, for cryin' out loud?!"

Now if you're like me, mine is loaded with various styles, shapes and sizes that were worn once and never worn again. They're either too tight, too low, too high, too chafing, give you wedgies, sag like an old hag, or keep fallin' down. So I shove them to the back of the drawer thinking in case of a "laundry emergency" if I have not one other pair or I go commando type of thing. It takes a long time to find a perfect brand and style that passes your comfort test and you have to suffer through a lot of cheap crap before you find the right one that satisfies you to no end…. Hmmm… underwear has a lot in common with finding a good man.

Well, I finally found a pair of panties that fit perfectly like a Goldilocks and the Three Bears kinda' moment, …. "it was juuuuuuust right." For two years I had no problem getting the same brand and style in the same store. Then one year it happened…. There was a clearance on all of them because the manufacturer was going out of business and they were never to be made again. My heart skipped a beat in sheer panic. I saw other women eyeing the bin of panties and I coveted that rack like Golum cooing, "my precious, my precious". I hysterically blurted out, "I'm buying them all, nothing for sale here, they're all mine," Like a freak I grabbed armloads of the stuff and ran for the check out.

I tried to figure out the math and how many years I could stretch them if I rationed them to myself on a quarterly basis. I would only throw one out if it's so worn and frayed to shreds that it's falling off of me. I have fond memories of a pink pair that gave faithful service for a few years and finally sacrificed itself so another could be worn. (Rest in Peace my friend) Hey, you get used to a favorite pair thinking of moments you've made while proudly flaunting them and so they're hard to give up and throw out, y'know?.

So the drawer gets bigger and bigger....it's such a drudgery to pull the drawer out and thin the herd. It's the one chore, outside the sock drawer (but I'll get to that) that we, as humans, put off. It's a pain in the butt and no-one likes to do it. Well....I suppose there are those freaks out there that have their underwear and sock drawers perfectly organized and the underwear is folded so a quarter could bounce off of it... I think they may be aliens from another dimensions so if your spouse has a perfectly folded and organized underwear drawer sorted by color, size, and occasion you might want to be careful. They might suck your brains out one night..... just sayin' ... watch your back.

Stay tuned for our next episode of "Dresser Drawers Gone Wild" as we delve into the secret world of socks... a whole other evil to "boot". ~ Smirk ~

~ SOCK IT TO ME! ~

I was struggling to get the kids ready for school one morning in my daily fun little game of "try and make the school bus" when it came down to the socks. Everyone's lunch was made, homework in their backpacks…. I can practically hear the rumbling of that clanking orange monster coming down the road when I look down and notice they both have bare feet – no socks or shoes. I make a mad dash back up the stairs for socks only to discover a hot mess of mismatches and no "pairs".

It's amazing to me that everyone's sock drawer is so stuffed you can't shut the drawer all the way but yet, ya' can never seem to find a decent pair to wear for some reason. A ton of them don't match, don't fit, don't feel good, or have holes or tar on them. I can't find the time to clean out the crap out of my own sock drawers let alone the kid's too. My son is 6 years old and he still has "18 month old" ones in there that obviously don't fit and are just gumming up the works.

I can't tell you how many pairs of holiday socks Grandma has gotten us. You got your St. Paddy's day green ones with cloverleaves, Valentine pink heart ones, Halloween spooky ghost ones, and of course the red and white candy cane Christmas ones. Unfortunately you only get to wear the things once a year and they just take up room the rest of the year. God forbid if I try to put a pair of Christmas socks on them in the spring. Only eight and my daughter knows a fashion faux pas when she sees one. "Mom, it's Easter, not Thanksgiving and they don't match – this one's a baby booty." "Just cause there's a turkey on them doesn't mean they're only for Thanksgiving – they could be the Easter Bunnie's helpers – the Easter turkey helper." She didn't buy it and that bus was barreling down the road so she got one white anklet with a hole and one white knee-high… at least they were the same color… her brother got one black one and one navy one – close enough in my book. So I shove them out the door and on their way.

I try to match them up in my weekly "Sock Game" as I call it. When all the socks of the entire family are done in the laundry I throw them altogether in a basket and save them for last. I throw the whole pile on the bed and me and the kids see who can get the most socks paired in a minute. There are some days though, that we're all too pooped after putting the regular clothes away to play the sock game and they sit in the basket as I promise myself I'll do them the next day. By the end of the week the basket is still sitting there and I've picked from it in my morning scramble to the point that only the ones left are the ones they say "don't feel good".

Lord, then it hits me – my mother wished this upon me when I was in 2nd grade and giving her hell about my socks. For some reason none of my socks ever "felt good" because the seam along the toe line always seemed to irritate me. I would make my mother cut the seams out of the socks before I'd agree to wear them. Of course by the end of the day my toes were sticking out the top because they came apart. It was such a daily tug of war with my mother and myself getting frustrated. "Someday, Carol Ann, you're gonna get this back with your own kids!" and I swear she laid a gypsy sock curse on me. "May all your offspring have problems with socks forever more causing grief to their mothers, I sayeth so!"

Well no wonder none of the socks match, or they have paint on them, or toe holes the size of a baby's head, or that the black socks always seem to fade at different rates so that some are kinda gray and the other one's are black but all pilly. It's because of some gypsy sock curse my mother put on me when I was 7 years old!

So I had an epiphany about all this and how I seem to have sock trouble with a capital "T". It's because of my mother. Poor mothers… basically everything comes down to the mother's fault it seems. I think about this for a minute as I watch my kids in karate class and stare down at my dress pants with one Buffalo Bill sock and one argyle sock peeking out of my shoes. Shaking my head and rolling my eyes I let out a deep sigh…my daughter will one day yell at me for ruining her life too I'm sure… her kids will probably want all the sock seams cut out… I heard it skips a generation.

~ IN CELEBRATION OF THE ALMIGHTY HAIR DRYER ~

If there ever was a major event in human history it would have to be the invention of the hair dryer! Amen to that, sister, hell yeah! The first hair dryer was actually the vacuum cleaner! Around 1890 the poor women were so frustrated with their hair they took to vacuuming it. Women dried their hair by connecting a hose to the exhaust of their vacuum cleaners. Can you believe that shit? Finally around 1920 some woman musta' yelled at her crazed inventor husband, "Damn it! That stupid belly button cleaner invention is just not gonna catch on I tell ya' — make me a contraption that can dry my @#$% hair!" Life just ain't right if a woman doesn't have her hair dryer to get her mane perfect. Guys just give up. "Nothin' a baseball cap can't cure," is the answer to most of their hair issues.

You know what I'm talkin' about. You and your hair dryer are as one; like wine and cheese;

Tom chasing Jerry; what Avon is to lipstick… you get the picture. Be good to your hair dryer and it will make you look like America's Next Top Model. Piss it off and you will be going to work with a headband or worse… a scrunchie.

It's exciting when you buy a new one and getting used to it… the feel for the handle… all its features of high vs. low… burning like the sun… or cool like a York Peppermint Patty. You'll get into a good groove and your hair will begin to respond like you were Rapunzel brushing long golden locks.

Ya' don't realize how important it is until you have to make do with a strange dryer. Like say you stay at a friend's house or go on vacation and have to use a substitute and wind up looking like a Rastafarian. No matter what you try it's just not happenin'. Your hair will part the wrong way, your child will accidentally call you Grandma ….The Little Rascal's "Alfalfa" comes to mind as you do battle with the most stubborn cowl. The Frizz Police are now pounding at your door and Lady Clairol is asking for a "before" picture. Inevitably someone, like your mother, will say, "Oh my God, I can't believe you went out in public lookin' like that!"

A good hair dryer that makes you look good and isn't expensive, and doesn't have an annoying buzzing sound is hard to find. Just like finding a mate you have to suffer through a few cheap crappy ones before you find the "one" that brings out your true beauty. It's sad when a good one finally goes kaput. You almost want to give it a proper burial in honor of the years you've been together. I've been with some of my hair-dryers longer than some of my past relationships. Like a gypsy psychic, when my hair dryer bursts into flames, starts to melt, and shorts out the whole house it usually means my relationship was also on the fritz. Bad hair day = relationship in the toilet.

I've used my hairdryer for so many things in my life. In the seventies my hair dryer was a good substitute for a .99mm as I pretended to be one of Charlie's Angels in my Wonder Woman underwear and braces. When needed in a pinch I've turned to it to hot wax my skis prior to a competition. I've used a hairdryer to heat up left-over pizza in a dorm room in a drunken stupor at 2 a.m. In my 20s when I froze my ass off in a dingy apartment in Buffalo (no heat) I turned to the hair dryer to keep me warm like I was the little "Match Girl". Only I hope they don't find me in a snow bank clutching my hair dryer frozen to death one day. That would suck. I have no idea why but out of all the Christmas specials that came around as a kid I always loved that one the most. Everyone else was hoping Rudolph the Red nosed reindeer was going to be on soon and there I was pining for the holiday special where the little girl dies in the end. Wow, now that's going off on a tangent. I should be named "Tangent Queen".

So, yes, the hair dryer can be used for most anything. In a spastic moment I've even used a hair dryer to get the wrinkles out of my silk blouse when the iron broke, and in a lazy moment blew dust-bunnies behind the furniture promising myself I was getting the vacuum cleaner out real soon to deal with this mess properly.

Y'know, I'm not the only one that relies on the hair dryer for comfort and support and perhaps a little mischief. My girlfriend, for instance, lives on a dangerous curve where people speed and scare the hell out of her and the kids. Out of fear and frustration she keeps threatening that she's gonna park her car in front of her house and sit in it pointing her hair dryer at on-coming cars pretending she's a cop checking people's speed with a radar gun.

Then just the other day I was watching a show on people's odd obsessions and one story was about a woman that has to have her hair dryer on the pillow next to hers or she can't go to sleep. Maybe she wants to be prepared in case of a middle of the night hair emergency… like if Brad Pitt suddenly climbed through her window looking for hair care products and a good Conair Power Boost with 200volts. Hey, ya never know.

So I think the hair dryer has proven its worth in the world of famous inventions and deserves its own holiday. So in celebration of the hair dryer I nominate to make it a holiday on the first day of August and call it, "Blow Heaven"…nah, sounds like a really bad drug porn… perhaps, "The day the earth was dry"…nope, too gloomy and apocalyptic …. How about "Got Hair?" No? Wait — I got it — "Dry-a-licious Day"! It has a ring to it, don'tcha think?

~ SUPERMARKET SOAP OPERA ~

Oy…. supermarkets. There's nothing like standing in the express lane with a lot of other people in front of you and the old lady at the front of the line is writing a check and yadda yadda yadda -it takes forever. It's like the equivalent of being behind a school bus in the morning.

Supermarkets are the soap opera of daily life. It's a place where all the women's magazines claim you can meet attractive men, but I've been going to markets my whole adult life and know this to be a crappy lie. Because I've actually believed this I've gone to the store on a Saturday night in a slinky dress wearing bright red lipstick only to find desperate women in the ice cream aisle and pathetic men in the beer aisle.

If I could get away with it I'd prefer to go at 10 p.m. in my filthy bathrobe and house slippers but don't want to risk it just in case the stupid magazine is right. I basically prefer to live life in my bathrobe. I wish I could walk around town in my bathrobe and slippers like the senile old lady down the street. Why she should she have all the fun? She keeps forgetting where she lives after going to the supermarket for the paper so she'll walk in a circle around my block for hours. After about thirty laps I finally yell out, "Ya missed it again, Edna!! You live in the red house!"

One thing that bugs me to death in supermarkets is the laundry detergent situation. They all claim to magically lift stains off of clothes. I'm talking tomato sauce, mud, tar, and blood. First of all if my shirt was covered with blood stains I don't think my first thought would be "Now which product will get out these nasty stains?" I think I'd be thinking about the stab wound that's currently putting those stains there in the first place. The only time I'd be worrying about blood stain removal is if I just killed someone myself and needed to clean away the evidence. In that case burning the damn shirt would be best rather than shopping for detergent. I mean you just killed someone — is the shirt really that important that you'd want to keep it?

The last time I went to the market I must have had a sign on my forehead that said, "If you're really weird please come up to me and start a conversation." As I was walking down one aisle I notice a man with about twenty of those gallon containers of water in his cart and he was still putting more in. He looks at me and very psychotically says, "I'm going to take a bath tonight." So I s-l-o-w-l-y back out of the aisle nodding my head trying not to make any sudden movements lest he whip out a bazooka and blow me away right into the tampon section. I don't think I'd like that written in my obituary in the local paper: "Woman looking for a date at the supermarket, dies amongst a pile of extra absorbent Tampax after taking a bullet to the chest region from a man wanting a bath." What a way to go.

Did you ever go on the "20 items or less express lane" with one item and start counting the items in the cart of the person in front of you and mentally start griping to yourself about the fact that they really have 24 items and who the hell do they think they are anyways? Oh, c'mon, admit it — we all do it. Just as sure as another day when we mentally convince ourselves we can go onto that lane ourselves because 25 cans of green beans should be counted as one item because it's the same product, never mind the fact that it's in 25 separate cans. Oh, and of course, when we turn around to see the woman with one item behind us mentally counting all those cans of green beans we give her a dirty look that says, "Step off, lady".

So it goes in the world of the Supermarket Soap Opera.

~ HOME PARTIES GONE WILD ~

It started in the 1950's with all those housewives having Tupperware parties, then came the Avon get-togethers, but now it has just plain gotten out of control, ladies! Everywhere you turn some friend is having a home party of food, lingerie, make-up, kitchen supplies — you name it. So to be polite you say you'll go but you think in the back of your mind that you are absolutely *not* gonna buy a thing. By the end of the night you've spent $100 on crap you really don't want and the representative is trying to talk you into hosting your own party as well. You know I'm right!

Let me just start by dissecting everything. You all know about my skewed background with cooking so let's just say that Pampered Chef is not my bag. Do I really need to buy a whisk for $85 when I can get one at Shop-rite for $2? How many times am I really going to use that whisk anyways, since my main staple is Lean Cuisine and Oreo's? That stuff is for the professional chef and more than likely I'd wind up using that whisk to comb my daughter's hair when she's late for the school bus and I can't find the hairbrush.

Let's see — what other home party products can I roast? Avon and Mary-Kay seem to be on the list. I'm not a big fan of make-up to begin with but do feel it's necessary at times — like when you have a big date or important work meeting and suddenly the largest crater pimple in the Guinness book of World Records decides to grow on your chin. So you dig through all the hundreds of dollars of crap you got talked into at the last Mary Kay party that made bold promises of banishing such things from your face, the planet, and possibly killing local wildlife only to discover — *they lied*! Next, you turn to good old Avon, the heavy-hitter, only to discover you have a whole purse full of those little tiny lipstick samples that your daughter used up on her dolls and the cover-up is just nowhere to be found. Why? Because if there's ever been an unspoken rule on this earth it's that you can never find something when you really need it the most. So in desperation you stop at the dollar store on your way to work to buy some cover-up and mascara hoping that maybe one or the other will distract everyone's attention from the obvious tumor on your face. Let me just comment that there are reasons why you don't buy those items (and also deodorant) from dollar stores. Trust me — you will have people handing you pamphlets on domestic violence and asking how long you've been a beaten housewife.

The latest craze appears to be "Tastefully Simple" parties. I went to one recently. I wasn't actually invited — I sorta crashed it drunk as a skunk and half-way through the presentation. How sad — back in the day I'd be crashing a bachelor party and now I'm crashing a food party of middle-aged women. (Sigh) The horror!

Anyways… I had just dropped off my kids with their father for the weekend, and after listening to my grandmother go on and on about how she wants to introduce my ex-husband to some nice girl because "he really deserves it," I just had to get out of the house. My girlfriend said she needed to make an appearance at a party and I'm all for it since I'd been dipping into grandpa's cough medicine and was finally getting my groove on and thinking it was gonna be a wild time. Suddenly I found myself at a very posh home filled with conservative upper class ladies at a "Tastefully Simple" party. Bad place to be if you're loaded with a bad case of the munchies. After shamefully gorging on all the chip, dip, salsa, bread, and dessert samples they asked what I wanted to order.

"Well, let's see, the salsas were too hot, and I'm going to start my diet so I don't want the brownies but, hey, that dip in the middle with the celery is amazing! I'll take a vat of that stuff," I gushed. The hostess just gave me a dirty look and said that was the only thing that wasn't from Tastefully Simple — it was just some dip from Shop-Rite they put with the celery. Then she asks if I want to host my own Tastefully Simple party and all I could think of to say was, "That would require me to actually have friends and I don't seem to have any of those at the moment." Well, I did just move there five months ago.

Yeah, I don't think I have to worry about being invited to anymore home parties anytime soon.

~ THE ADULT SIPPY CUP ~

Ahhh... the sippy cup. What a great invention; how I love it so. It comes in several fun colors and has saved my couch and carpet from grape juice disasters on several occasions. You get attached to it and even when your toddler is ready for an open cup without a top you're terrified to let them take that next step even though they REALLY need to graduate to a regular cup or glass. Just thinking about all the spills on the furniture, floors, clothes, and other siblings makes you want to cringe. They may be ready but I'm not. If you've ever seen a six or eight year old child in the store drinking from a sippy cup, which is waaaaay over the sippy cup drinking age limit - they're mine. So when you give an odd look to the mother and think, "What the hell is wrong with that woman?" it's probably me. I'm in total denial trying to avoid the open cup at all expenses.

The invention of the juice box doesn't make it any easier either. It makes me even lazier than the sippy cup. The path of least resistance – just toss them a square box with its own straw attached and you're done. You avoid having to take out some gallon jug of juice, finding a clean cup, pouring it, and then finding a paper towel to clean up the spill you just made. All hale the juice box!

Do we ever really outgrow the juice box or sippy cup though? The adult version of the juice box is the big box of wine you get in the liquor store. My mother and her gal pal cousins love the thing so much I put an enormous straw coming out of the top of it, covered it in tinfoil and wrote, "Adult Juice

Box" on the front of it. They laughed and scolded me at the same time as mother's always do. I'm middle-aged and she's still shaking her head with a smirk muttering, "Damn kids".

Now if they could just shrink down the BIG wine box into individual containers with their own straws attached it would be a hit with my mom and her cackling, red and purple hat wearin', cougars. They would buy it in 6-packs, start a trend and maybe it could land them on the cover of AARP magazine.

The Adult version of the sippy "cup" is the travel mug. I'm addicted to travel mugs I will confess and have several in a variety of designs that has now become excessive enough to call it a "collection" like coca-cola memorabilia. I had a friend over recently for a chat and I made us a pot of coffee and served it to him in a travel mug instead of a coffee cup. He sheepishly said, "It's in a travel mug – are you telling me to leave?" It seemed natural to me since I use them for everything but to him I was a bad hostess.

What's not to like about a travel mug? I don't have to worry about spilling and scalding myself, it keeps cold liquids cold and hot liquids hot for a long time. If I put it in a mug it gets cold quick and they don't hold much – kinda like a shot glass of coffee; and after all that work of fixing it with milk and sugar it doesn't seem worth the effort. I need something much bigger than a typically small cup that lets the coffee get cold. What better way to have coffee but in the travel mug which is big, will keep it hot longer, and can hold up to two normal cups worth? It's a no brainer in my book. Although my friend found it a bit odd...

I just recently stocked up on some new ones to add to my collection of travel mugs that I now consider my fine china. That just about makes every southern redneck proud of me right now and I'm sure to receive "welcome to the family" cards this week. (I draw the line at putting broken washing machine and couches in my front yard though.) One of my favorite new travel mugs is one of the old lady cartoon character "Maxine" because when you hit a button on the bottom she says irate and slightly perverse comments about speeding down the road while drinking coffee. I'm pretty sure if I used these flippant comments geared towards policemen pulling you over for speeding the next thing I would hear would be, "Ma'am, get out of the car and put your hands above your head,". Maybe I can just hit the button and the recording can be blamed for what I was thinking anyways. Hmmm... better not be tempted.... I should just take one on the road that won't get me into trouble... like the one with the Buffalo Bills on it will just get the cop to laugh uncontrollably and he'll offer me condolences.

~ LET THE GAMES BEGIN! ~

It's that time of year when the local school kids have a week of "Field Day" doing such feats of sporting challenges such as the egg toss, sack race, jump rope competition, and crab walk relay races. Everyone always won a ribbon even if you didn't win. I can't tell you how many "participant" ribbons I received in those elementary school years. Of course they were never the striking royal blue color of the first place, or the bold red ribbons of second place — nope, they were the crap brown ribbon of the loser that they felt sorry for. I was proud of them until I realized they were the equivalent of finding a severed finger in your onion soup.

After that I was determined to get one of those blue ribbons even if I had to play dirty. Since I was the size of an oompa loompa I set my sights on something I thought I had a shot at: the sack race. That itchy burlap and 50 feet of lawn was my one claim to fame and notoriety amongst the 9 year old hard core athletes of the fourth grade. I watched and waited for my turn to pounce on this esteemed challenge of jumping inside of something that read, "Corn Feed". I was so small I just pulled it up to my chin and shot off like a Mexican jumping bean lit on tequila. I actually won the stupid thing and that was about the gist of my 15 minutes of fame until the following year when I had to defend my "title".

A new girl from the Bronx moved to our community and after hearing of my incredible win decided she was gonna knock me off my pedestal. We stood next to each other at the starting line and eyed each other up with fierce grit and determination. The little pop gun went off and I broke a sweat in my pink overalls and lucky "Hello Kitty" underpants. That's right, baby, don't mess with me in a dark alley if I've got my lucky "Hello Kitty" underpants on! So there we were, sack to sack, elbowing each other in the gut, pulling on each other's pig tails and frothing at the mouth like a rabid bear jazzed up on honey. I beat her by one pinky toe and retained my school record as she suffered the agony of defeat falling at the last minute because of a shoe lace malfunction.

Did you know there are many types of Field Days in the world? Apparently it was a term coined in the 1700's when the military decided to do a day of field maneuvers with periodic intervals of eating, drinking and blowing crap up. So the term "field day" came from that — although I personally think "Blowing Crap Up Day" would have sounded more enticing. Since that time there are now all different types of field days in the U.S. such as: Farmer's Field day, Math Field Day, Radio Field Day, and Woodsmen's Field Day. Yeah, I know — definitely very exciting I imagine.

Farmer's field day consists of a variety of events such as agricultural mechanics, vegetable crop identification, tractor races, and animal management competition. Woo Hoo! I don't think I can stand the suspense of watching a couple of old coots race around with a pig strapped to their backs. It must be very exciting to watch the frustrated brow of the fledgling rookie farmer struggling between guessing if it's a piece of corn or a rutabaga in a kill all game of "name that crop".

And what sick person thought of Math Field Day? My brain hurts just thinking about such a concept. The way I figure it is that all I need to know about math is how much 25% off that cute skirt at Penney's comes out to.

I'm not even going to touch Radio Field day because that's just a bunch of strange people sitting around with a ham radio testing their emergency broadcast systems and eating Dinty Moore stew in their bomb shelters like it's a tail gate party for their favorite football team. Go Ham! Yeah!

Now the Woodsmen Field Day is amazing! Sometimes you can catch one of these competitions on some obscure channel when nothing else is on. These people are totally cuckoo bananas. They nearly take off various body parts in chainsaw carving competitions, axe throwing (Good Lord!), climbing up greased telephone poles in 10 seconds (now that's a good skill if you're getting chased by a mountain lion) and of course the log rolling contest whereby you try not to fall off the log and into the river. That last one is really funny if you have the "chicken dance" playing in the background as they battle for the title of Log Master. I wonder if the grand prize is a year's supply of Hungry Jack TV dinners.

Well, at any rate, for all those competing in a sport, math, farm, radio or lumberjack field day may you take home the top prize to boast forevermore that you are the King or Queen of tossing an egg, completing a math problem in 10 seconds, shearing a sheep in 5, whistling the anthem on a ham radio or chopping a piece of wood to look like Aunt Betty! Let the games begin!

~ FOR WHOM DOES THE DENTIST'S DRILL WHIR? ~

So I finally went to the "Dentist" after waiting a whole flippin' year for an appointment. Yup… whole year. *That* booked. Why in God's name would anybody want to be breaking down the door to the dentist's office I have no idea. Just the mere thought of having to go to one, kinda gives you that same pit in your stomach you get when you have to go to the gynecologist. Ya' just can't help but grumble, wince a fake smile, and try not to be so cranky and nasty that you get thrown outta the place.

There's just nothin' all that good you can say about the dentist's office. Teeth cleaning? Mm.. not too bad I guess. Cavities? Nah.. mildly uncomfortable but not afraid of those really, no…. The sound of the drill and Root Canals? Oh, hell, yeah! I'd rather be struck by lightning. I don't care how old ya' are – when you hear that drill go off ya' tend to cringe and tell yourself, "Oh…crap…this is really gonna suck."

It's also because it costs more than a small island in St. Thomas to get one. It always baffles me how insurance companies just pretend that teeth aren't part of the human body …..they consider them more like an optional accessory – like a pair of earrings. Another thing I hate about root canals is how you have to go through three or four appointments before the cap is on and it's done with. After the fourth appointment my mouth feels like it was stretched two sizes and I could probably be mistaken for a wide mouth bass.

It's so nice that they wear masks now because, *man*, do they ever get sooo close to your face! I'm sorry but that just creeps me out…well…unless they're super smokin' hot like George Clooney. {wink accompanied by a sly smirk} As a kid I had this dentist in Jersey that didn't wear a mask and if he could get his whole face halfway down my throat in pursuit of some cavity he would. He had the worst breath ever to boot! It baffled me how a dentist could have bad breath. That's like a hair stylist with hair that looks like it was done with the weed whacker – just doesn't instill much confidence in their services. As a matter of fact the whole place just had this medicine-y, formaldehyde type scent to it whenever you crossed the threshold. It hits you like a Listerine pie to the face. I'm pretty sure it's a chemical compound used to instantly cause paralyzing fear in all those that dare to enter … <<<dun dun dun>>>…. "The Dentist's Lare". Must make it easier to control the real screamers and biters if they're half out of it -- stunned into obedience by formaldehyde.

So, here I am taking my children to the dentist, trying to make it a "fun and positive" experience for them when all along I'm breaking a sweat like a Pavlovian dog at the mere utterance of the word "dentist". I didn't have the best experiences as a child, which is probably where it stems from. For some reason or other all my baby molars started jumpin' ship too early and this really nasty dentist decided to put all these metal crowns on them to make sure they stayed in longer. Boy was he ticked off when I was back a week later with a Sugar Daddy full of crowns. He shook his head mumbling something about candy being the bane of his existence. He took his frustrations out on me I swear – just drove those caps straight down to the bone cursing under his bad breath the whole time.

By far though, my worst experience was one Christmas Eve a few years back when I was in terrible agony with a toothache. It was after hours, during a snow storm no less and I still had to drive three hours to my family home for the holidays. After many calls I finally found one dentist that would see me. Turns out I needed an emergency root canal and it was infected as well. "Now make sure you take this pain killer within the hour because the Novocain is going to wear off and it's really going to hurt," he says. "Won't that make me drowsy? I have to drive for three hours," I reply. That's when *HE* winced. So there I was driving for hours after the Novocain wore off in agony and without a narcotic in sight. I felt like I got hit in the face with a sledge-hammer…repeatedly… like Lizzie Borden givin' me 40 whacks kinda' repeatedly! I'm pretty sure all the people I sped past in a screaming rage to get home thought I was a stalker on a mad killing spree.

My mother answered the door and took one look at me and said, "Holy smokes, what happened to you?! Were you hit by a car?! Did someone mug you?!" I felt like a little Tiny Tim in the snow at her door. All I could do was pathetically sputter in a whispery, slurred tone ...."Vicodin"!!!!!

~ THE PLIGHT OF THE
THUMB SUCKER ~

Braces! That one word causes a shiver down the spine of your hardcore thumb-sucker knowing the end to their guilty pleasure is at hand. Now most kids naturally give up sucking their thumb around the age of two to three years but then there are the feisty ones that hang in there till they are staring down an orthodontist like a western show-down not giving up without a fight. I, myself, never sucked my thumb, oddly enough, but others around me have suffered the consequences resulting in a mouth full of metal.

My cousin Sue Anne, sucked her thumb until she was thirteen years old and was forced to give it up by barbaric methods. Poor Aunt Marie tried everything to get her daughter to stop. Sue Anne would come over to play and have some sort of new attempt upon her thumbs that Aunt Marie contrived. One day Sue Anne had band-aids on her thumbs but then she sucked those off in her sleep and nearly choked to death. Then Aunt Marie put cayenne pepper in Sue Anne's nail polish and then had her dip her thumbs in Tabasco sauce but all that did was wake up the teenager to liking spicy Mexican food.

I'll never forget having a sleep over at her place marveling at the oven mitts that were duct-taped to her pajamas thinking "poor Sue Anne"… ahhh but later on it got quite entertaining for the rest of us cousins to see her chewing the thumbs off the oven mitts in her sleep like a rabid animal. I think we even took "Polaroid's" of it. Oooh… a pre-historic way to take a picture way before Smartphones.

So the orthodontist was called in like some sort of modern day Dr. Frankenstein as a last resort to break Sue Anne of her thumb sucking way. Back then they rigged up the most horrific torturous contraption on the inner part of some heavy metal 1970's braces that looked like you had a whole train track in there. The end of the line for a thumb sucker was a row of needle sharp pins secured to the back of those train track braces that acted like barbed wire to any trespassing thumb. But God bless her little heart little Sue Anne gave it a shot now and then and she'd wake up in the morning with her thumb covered in little bloody dots from all the times she got stuck by the pins. I hope she can laugh about it now but, Holy Crow, back then she was NOT happy about it I can say for sure. {Smirk}

So this silly old memory is brought to mind this week as I consult with an orthodontist about what to do with one of my own children's thumb sucking ways and impending braces if the habit isn't nipped in the bud. He recommended this great handy dandy new device called a "Thumb Guard" that's supported by doctors everywhere…. Yadda yadda. Holy smokes it's this odd looking piece of PVC bolted to their little thumbs like a cast that makes them look like they're always hitch-hiking. With its bolted leather straps that come with a lock and key that only parents can open it comes complete with a money back guarantee because they're positive it'll do the trick…. Oh and it's a cajjillion of course. Funny I can't remember getting into a time machine to medieval times and torture devices. I suppose it was an improvement from the 1970's sharp prongs.

"Add to cart." I can always use it as a unique conversation starter when she chews it off in a week. "Oh, what a unique sculpture thing you have there, Carol, it looks like a thumb - where-ever did you find it?" "On the side of a highway in Texas hitchin' a ride."

~ DISNEY OR BUST! ~

Has anyone NOT been to Walt Disney World? It seems to be one of those obligations whereby the typical family unit takes the long journeyed pilgrimage to worship a mouse for a week's time. If you have kids you just can't escape this inevitable trek as if you were on a hunt for the Holy Grail. So I had this crazy idea that I should just bite the bullet and do it: a whole week at Disney just myself and my two children under the age of six. One friend said, "My God, you're brave! Alone with two pre-schoolers at Disney?! I wouldn't even go alone with my husband!" I didn't realize until I was battling my way to Newark airport and going through security with a stroller what I had gotten into. How on earth am I going to make it there and back and not lose one of these kids is beyond me, I thought. I had visions of some strange foreign man offering me $10 grand for one of the kids. "How much for the little six year old girl? She will make a good wife for my grandfather." I almost had a panic attack every time they let go of my hand.

I'm glad I made the decision to fly there even though it cost a fortune. My parents decided to drive the two day trip down there when I was a kid and take the dog with us too. Can you imagine?! A station wagon loaded with kids, a cranky grandmother, and a whiney dog with a bladder problem — for TWO DAYS? Along the way they saw some rotted out pioneer wagon wheels and strapped them to the wagon's roof so we definitely looked like a Chevy Chase family movie. We also decided to stop at the South of the Border for some illegal fireworks, of course. After buying enough explosives to rival any local terrorist everyone loaded back into the family truckster and started back down the highway. About 20 minutes later somebody said, "Where's the dog?" After thinking hard for a few minutes somebody said, "Carol was out walking her I think." Another minute passed before they realized I wasn't in the car either. Can you believe they actually thought about the dog missing prior to their own child? All I know is that I'm walking the dog and suddenly I see them doing 90mph straight for me in a cloud of smoke screeching to a stop and angrily yelling out the window, "Where the hell have you been? Get in this car right now!" Then it hit me they actually left me at the South of the Border! "Did you forget me, mom?" "We most certainly did not and keep this attitude up and they'll be no Mickey Mouse for you, young lady!"

I fondly remember going to Disney World as a child and loving all the rides, eating a ton of ice cream, and getting one of those loveable black mouse ear hats. As an adult, it cost me a week's pay for those damn mouse ears (which are already crushed at the bottom of the closet), and I roasted an hour in line dealing with temper tantrums not only from my kids but everyone else's — all for a three minute ride. At least when you walked the blazing asphalt around this money-sucking playground there was some sort of water sprinkler that would mist the crowd now and then. I found myself standing for 10 minutes next to an 8 foot tall coke bottle that sprayed every 80 seconds. I didn't want to move from that spot. Now if those Disney people were really smart they'd hook it up to spray pina coladas, making the adults happy and more tolerant of their screaming little angels. I can't tell you how many frustrated adults were speaking through clenched teeth, "You're just lucky we're in public!"

What are the two most important things you need on any vacation? A camera and clean underwear usually top the list. Well, I forgot both. So I had to buy those "throw away" cameras" and search for a Wal-Mart. Couldn't find a department store anywhere to save my life. So while at Disney I wanted to buy them t-shirts and happen to see they had 3-pks of underpants. Guess how much two shirts and two packs of panties cost me at Disney? Put your drink down and swallow your food because I don't want you to choke. Now I knew it would be pricey but I almost needed a defibrillator when they said, "$76.00 please." I almost spit out my teeth yelling, "For two kids t-shirts and underpants?!" Can you believe that crap?! Yesterday I overheard my son saying to his cousin, "My momma says my underpants are laced with gold." Got that right.

All in all it was a bit trying at times but had its fun moments too. I will say I definitely deserve a 'Mother of the Year' Award and absolutely knocked off some time in purgatory. I'm gonna get a t-shirt that reads, "I made it through a week alone at Disney with 2 kids". I'm fear-less! I can do anything now! If someone tells me they climbed Mount Everest I'll just sneer, "Pshaw…... that's nothin!"

~ CAMPING UP A THUNDERSTORM ~

So I finally decided to give in to my children's heartfelt desire to go camping; to sleep on the ground with insects, eat food blackened from a campfire, and get a wilderness patch on my Mommy uniform. I figured if I could survive a week at Disney alone with them I could probably handle putting up a tent and splitting wood. Others weren't so sure, "You're a better man than I am," said my ex-husband, as he kissed his children goodbye hoping he'd see them alive again. His idea of camping is going to the Holiday Inn instead of the Hilton. Putting a piece of tarp in a wooded area is just one notch above being homeless according to him. So off I went to the wilds of Pennsylvania in search of a campground that the internet promised me would be a good time. Course I didn't count on the rain and the traffic and getting there in the pitch dark.

Now during the week my father had already set up the tent in his backyard to show me how to take it down, assuming I could put it back up the same way. Just in case, I took a picture of it on my digital camera so I could refer back to it if need be. I was feeling pretty confident taking it down with him as it seemed to go smoothly and I timed it at 10 minutes worth of effort. "This is a snap," I thought, "I am woman, hear me roar; I can do anything." Somehow 10 p.m. Friday night putting the thing up in the pitch dark in a thunderstorm with two little ones whining in that high pitched tone that makes you want to eat your own young…. Well…. let's just say that's "Mission Impossible III". When I was finished an hour later, it didn't look anything like the picture and unfortunately when I put it under the tree to keep dry I accidentally put the tent entrance right up against the tree and we couldn't get into it. Yup… had to take it all back down, turn it around, and put it back up again. "When you kids are teenagers and complain that I never took you anywhere or did anything I want you to remember this so I didn't suffer for nothin'!" I grunted, pounding in stakes with an axe almost hitting myself in the forehead with the blade and getting sopping wet in the process. It's amazing that no matter how well you prepare for camping, inevitably everything gets wet and musty.

Now it's been a decade or more since I've had the pleasure of sleeping on the hard ground and didn't mind it too much at first but by the third night I was asking the campground if they had complimentary chiropractic services so I didn't have to go home crippled. They failed to see the humor in that question which is surprising for people that worship a groundhog. Maybe they're cranky because of all their guests telling them, "It didn't say anything in the brochure about my campsite being located right next to a train that rumbles by every two hours blaring its whistle." That was, indeed, a little scrumptious tidbit we discovered at midnight just as the last blood we had was being donated to the local mosquito population. I also was surprised by the abundance of owls that hooted all night like there was a "Who" concert goin' on. I tried to frighten them off with a little child psychology, yelling, "Hmm…. Now where did I put my gun?" but apparently these owls were smarter than their New York cousins. It did, however, finally get the rowdy people at the next tent to turn the music off and go to sleep though.

So we roasted hot dogs in all their nitrate goodness, tested the diabetic waters with toasted marshmallows, did some swimming, told some ghost tales, cursed our sunburn, and overall had a pretty good time stumbling through a typical American pastime. "Mommy, can we do this again really soon?!" they shouted with excitement as I started the three hour drive back. "Sure thing," I said, "I'll tell your father to book the Holiday Inn for next month."

~ TIME TO PULL OUT
THE FAT CLOTHES! ~

Most people have what they call a "Spring/Summer" wardrobe and a "Fall/Winter" wardrobe. I have my "skinny" clothes and my "fat" clothes. Well, who are we kiddin' here, my "skinny" clothes graduated to the "Not TOO bad" clothes when I hit 38. I'm always twenty pounds up or twenty pounds down. That's my fat window. It used to be a smaller window like the one in the attic, but now it's a big ass bay window protruding out of the living room for all to see. Lately my fat clothes have graduated to "maternity" clothes as I try to convince myself that it's okay to still wear my old maternity clothes even though my kid is now four years old.

Pretty much every woman has a "fat wardrobe" but their confidence in their "skinny clothes" range through the ages from the "My Girls Night Out Clothes" in your twenties, the "Yeah, that's right, I'm a MILF and I can rock this minivan" thirties wardrobe, to the forties decade workin' the "Stella's got her groove back" wardrobe. Then you hit the laid back sixties, with "To hell with skinny clothes, I'm just gonna walk around in my underwear now" and the inevitable later years wandering around and mumbling, "Clothes? What clothes? Not wearin' any."

Like most Americans I swear I'm finally going to get in shape and stay that way. I'll join a gym, start dieting and get into the "skinny" clothes in the spring time but by October the cold weather sets in and so do the pounds. All those harvest apple pies, stews and raiding your kid's Halloween candy makes ya' feel warm all over. Then it's just a hop, skip and a jump to Thanksgiving and the endless amounts of feasting. Days of leftovers parade in as you make turkey soup, turkey dumplings, turkey pot pie and get all turkey-ied out, of course. Then it's a straight crapshoot to Christmas and all the other December holidays. Just thinking the words, "Holiday Cookie Swap" makes my cholesterol level spike up like the tree in Rockefeller Center. You're now heavily into the fat clothes as you buffet your way through all those Holiday parties and before you know it the school is asking you to be Mrs. Claus at their Festival of Lights event. So on New Year's Eve your resolution this year (and let's face it — EVERY year) is to get back in shape. You've almost convinced yourself to get back into it and give that diet a go but then Valentine's Day hits and like Al Pacino in "The Godfather" you're yelling to the refrigerator at midnight, "I try to get out but they just pull me back in." The nail in the coffin is that rat "Peter Cottontail" and all his Easter chocolaty promises.

Bikini season starts to beckon however and I finally make a real pledge to get into those skinny clothes. I buy into the latest craze that makes glorious promises with their incredible weight loss claims and buying $800 bucks of their packaged food. "Just eat all this delicious and nutritious gourmet food like we tell you and you'll lose a ton of weight and look like America's Next Top Model." You get a bunch of powdered packages with these incredible pictures of decadent, saucy heavenly foods on the box covers. With crossed fingers and praying for a miracle you zap the plate of stuff hoping that when the microwave "dings", out will pop a four course meal of roasted turkey and all the fix-in's. I keep thinking of Milla Jovonavich in "The Fifth Element" with Bruce Willis as she pops in a plate of powder, zaps it for 10 seconds, and she pulls out a hot steamy roast. "Chick-un good" she says in broken English. Unfortunately no such luck in my reality. By this time I feel like a "Biggest Loser" contestant and want to eat one of the other contestants.

So this year I decided to break this vicious cycle and change direction in my pursuit to live a healthy balanced lifestyle and just have ONE decent wardrobe that is not my maternity clothes, nor the clothes I have to starve to death to fit into. I'm not going to overeat through the holidays nor am I going to try every fad diet out there just so someone will kiss me when the ball drops on New Year's Eve. No more sufficing only on pills that make me look like a smokin' hot model but were banned for fear of death. No more diets of grapefruits and cabbage soup with the aftermath of massive amounts of gas that could explode a small village in India. No more dieting and binging till my hair falls out and everyone mistakes me for Sinead O'Connor. So what am I going to do different in my pursuit of attaining a size 5 life and *staying* there? Start exercising? Eating super healthy? Hell no! I'm gonna do what every other cougar does – I'm gonna start investing in liposuction and plastic surgery. I'll go into the coffin at 70 lookin' like I'm 20 and I won't have to suffer to do it. Now gimme some of that pie!!

~ BACK TO SCHOOL ~

Well all the little kiddie-do's went back to school this week. You could almost hear the collective sigh of relief peppered with a little sadness through-out the region as parents everywhere put those little ones on the bus with a tear in the eye and a lump in their throats. Half hour later what sounded like thunder was not your local weather but rather the grumblings of every teacher as they dealt with classes of crying kindergarteners and swearing teenagers. God bless those poor things as they struggle to help guide our offspring – I know I couldn't do it.

The fact that I kept my two children alive to the point of school-age is a miracle in itself. Ingrained upon my memory was holding my colicky daughter at three weeks of age and crying along with her thinking, "Why on earth did I do this to myself?" Five years later, with saggy body parts, ten more wrinkles and the loss of just about every hair on my head, I have to remind myself that in the end it is worth it. Ninety percent of child-rearing is living hell but the other ten percent is so wonderful it keeps you from jumping off the bridge.

The fact that I've passed my bad habits onto my little mini-me, like swearing better than any truck driver, is a mute point. "It was bound to happen in her teens, anyway," I reason. I fondly remember the first time my little darling picked up on this odd new slang of expressing one's anger. We were driving in the "mama mini-van" (always said I would never buy a mini-van) when another driver cut me off in a very near miss. Without thinking I yelled, "You Asshole!" From her car seat my darling child, holding onto her ducky for dear life, asked, "Mommy, why did you call him that?" So I begin to answer her, "Well, you see he ran a red light and red means stop…." and just when I was beginning to wonder why I was explaining traffic laws to a toddler, wouldn't you know it but yet another car runs a stop sign and pulls out onto the road in front of me and I have to slam on my brakes to avoid a collision. Without missing a heart beat I hear a little voice yell out, "Look, Ma, there's ANOTHER Asshole!" Got a quick wit, I'll give 'er that.

So all of this came to mind as the school bus rumbled down the road and with a big smile, I stood alongside my own mother and took pictures of her getting on the school bus and waved a tearful goodbye. I ponder what experiences my daughter will encounter in this year and all the wonders her little mind will absorb and breathe a sigh of relief that she has a good teacher to guide her. Someone that will help un-do all the mistakes I've made thus far and set her on a steady path of good manners, education and ambition. The glow of the moment ended abruptly however when my mother, filled with the unique ability to inflict catholic guilt on everyone she knows, says "I just don't see why you just can't home school."

~ HERE COMES THE SCHOOL BUS! ~

Riding the school bus is a rite of passage most of us face in life. Who doesn't remember the slow bumpy ride, the stench of diesel and old sneakers, an AC that never worked, those stupid windows that were impossible to get up or down without hurting your fingers, and the horrible sounds of grinding gears like it was being gutted by a serial bus killer?

Did anyone ever have a "nice" bus driver? In grade school I had a grizzly bear of a woman that musta' been 102 years old. Her name was "Faith" which is ironic considering nobody had any faith in her to get us to school and home alive and in one piece. Her middle name was "Hope" - another irony since ya' didn't have any of that either. She terrified the life out of us flying by on two wheels around those twisty country roads. Those two beady eyes with coke bottle glasses would glare at you from her overhead mirror as she yelled her bloody little head off to sit down and shut up or she was gonna pull over and come back there, dammit! (They can't do all that yellin' and threaten' so much nowadays since they got those cameras on board that make for interesting fodder on late night talk shows.) This shriveled up prune of a woman would yank that bus over and come barreling down the aisle with such fierceness that you barely had time to scribble a message to your parents where you think she could have buried your body.

Making the bus to begin with and not missing it is another whole evil right there. I remember my own mother running out after us in her ratty bathrobe and 50's curlers frantically waving a piece of burnt toast, yelling, "Wait, you forgot your breakfast!" I'd slink down in the seat pretending not to know her. "Who me? No, I have no idea who that lunatic woman is… I don't have a mother … I was hatched."

Now that I have my own children, every morning it's like a freaky game of Russian Roulette in a crazed rush to make that stupid school bus. I think the amount of stress suffered at this daily torture routine rivals being shocked with 3,000 volts. Like an umpire I yell "BUSSSSSSSSSS!!!" as I see it comin' down the road. I imagine the neighbors are sick of hearing me screaming like a crazy person down the driveway, "LET'S GO! MOVE IT! YOU'RE GONNA MISS THE BUS!! WHERE'S YOUR OTHER SHOE??!!! NO – YOU ARE NOT WEARING THAT! I practically shove my little darlings into the road thanking the Lord for school.

Boy, I can't tell you how many times the kids forgot something and I had to rush out after them in my PJ's totally humiliating my young in front of their friends. There I'd be running down the road, breakin' a sweat, in my "Mommy Needs Sleep" nightshirt flagging down the bus, "Wait, you forgot your snack!!" and waving a Scooby Doo Lunch box. They should have a huge net or wagon attached to the back of the bus so that all the parents sprinting down the road after the bus can whip the forgotten lunches, backpacks, and book reports in there. The kids won't get embarrassed and it'd save time.

Believe it or not, I actually was a bus driver once, right after college. The job posting read: "Former experience as a prison guard would be helpful". I now believe that diffusing a bomb would be a much less stressful position. The amount of spit balls I took out of the back of my head each day amounted to 10 pounds of loose leaf paper. The amount of trees that died just to be wadded up into a ball and pelted at my head would have made a Native American Indian cry in a commercial. I naively envisioned a happy experience with the kids singing that joyous popular song, "The wheels on the bus go round and round".

I will admit though I wasn't the best bus driver either. Not really bad like that bus driver currently in the news texting while he was driving the bus… more like I was starving and made a quick pit-stop at the McDonald's drive thru. Hey, at least I got fries for all the kids too. Unfortunately the bus didn't clear the overhang and it got stuck. Eventually I rammed my way through it and lucky for me nobody at the school noticed the scraped up, dented roof. Another job I totally sucked at.

I think it's safe to say in our society the School Bus has had significance in of our lives from our own childhood, experiencing it again with our own children, and maybe for some such as myself experiencing it from the driver's perspective. So respect the bus…. after it…it's the only time a kid will be in a motor vehicle without asking, "Are we there yet?"

~ HOMEWORK HELL ~

Now that my daughter is in second grade her homework is starting to get more difficult. Prior to this helping her was a snap — color in a few trees, write your alphabet and that was that. Now it's word problems and adding multiple numbers and I think I'm whining more than her. I just gotta say it — I couldn't stand doing homework the first time around, let alone twenty years later when I've burnt half my brain cells. When I finally finished college I felt free at last. Nobody told me about the fact that eventually I'd have to help my offspring. I feel robbed; cheated; like someone did a 'bait and switch' on me!

I sulk just thinking about the piles of work this kid is bringing home. I dread having to unzip that backpack each night — its barely been two months into the school season and it looks like it's been to war. I hate to admit it but some nights after a long day at work I say, "Oh to hell with it — we'll do it in the morning." Then like a madwoman I have to wake the poor kid up at the crack of dawn to do word problems. "If Billy has 8 apples and Jane has 7 apples but then Sara eats 2 and Billy whips 1 at Jane's head for stealing 3 of his and then Jack gets in on it and stomps 4 of them into applesauce, how many do they have left?" … and blah blah blah I could just shoot myself. This is why calculators were made, people. So we don't have to hurt our brains trying to figure out that everyone just needs to get along and go bake a pie.

Then there's the notes home: "Her biggest issue lately is her handwriting skills." Man it's like someone hit the rewind button on my life! I distinctly remember my teachers saying the same thing about me. Being a lefty they kept making me twist my arm around the top of the page and slant it to the right like all the righties. I wouldn't do it and reasoned that the righty's should slant right and the lefty's should slant left and not cripple themselves with a lifetime of carpel tunnel to conform to the righty way of life. Apparently back then they forced you to do it or suffer the wrath of the wooden ruler practically breaking your little hand altogether (if a teacher did that today she's be on death row). When my parents were called in for a conference about my refusal to slant the way of the righties I got a major talking to by all three of them about the proper way to write and how I won't amount to anything if I didn't have good penmanship. Like it was yesterday I remember with perfect clarity being quite flippant in my response, "Well, no one can read a word of the doctor's handwriting and he turned out okay and besides, twenty years from now none of this will matter." God, when I think about the nerve I had as a kid! Heavens!

As they get older it's gonna be sad when the teacher sends home notes saying, "Please check her homework" and I have to write one back saying that I did and thought it was all correct. Let's face it, I'm no Jeopardy contestant… unless you count the week they have all the grammar school kids on… I tend to get one or two correct that week.

Man, just the thought of future years of homework with all the things I hated the first time around is making me break out in hives. I can't remember all the crap they taught back then. My range for history stretches as far as the Pinto, the Nina and the Santa Marina. My take on science extends to rubbing a balloon on my head and sticking it to the wall. When it's time for calculus I'm just gonna have to tell 'em they're on their own.

All this homework leads to lots of questions I just don't have time to think about like, "Where does electricity come from?" and unfortunately they're no longer satisfied with my answer of "the wall." Suddenly I have to explain the whole Ben Franklin Kite n' Key deal which leads to discussions on the weather and thunder and lightning and it just never ends. "But HOW, Mommy? How?" is said over and over again like peeling an onion till you just want to scream "Just because, that's why!" "Yeah, but Mooooooommmmmmmmmyyyyy, if thunder makes that rumble sound from the lightning, then where does the lightning come from?" I contemplate delving into the whole build up of electron thing for a moment and finally just give up in frustration. "Y'know, sweety, that's a great question to ask your teacher tomorrow," I say, smirking, knowing full well I'm throwing the poor woman under the bus and my child will haunt them about it for the whole day. Thinking about the two hours of homework I just did with them all I can say is "Touché."

~ A JUNK DRAWER LIFE ~

"My life is a junk drawer," I mumble to myself as I rifle through the one drawer in the kitchen that all of us have rightly christened, "The Junk Drawer". On the hunt for a loose rubber band to tie around the handful of loose colored pencils all over the floor, I stumble upon the Kohl's receipt I was looking for last month and held on to it to shove in my wallet if I can ever find it in my purse. I've tried many a time to straighten out this black hole of a drawer where all the things you don't know what to do with end up....and who can organize such odds and ends?

What category would you put a couple of Barbie shoes you might find the other one to someday? Half the battle is the stacks of Campbell's labels and box tops you save for the school, some broken knick-knack you're going to glue back together if only you could find the glue in the drawer to begin with. Let's not forget a lost crayon, paper clips, an occasional safety pin, pencils, pens, coupons, baby pictures, pizza and Chinese food menus, and a zillion other odds and ends. Unfortunately rifling through this mess I cut my finger on the letter opener I tore the place apart last week looking for and it came back to bite me.

Now I grouchily go tackle my Junk Medicine Cabinet trying to find a band-aid. "Why can't I ever find anything I'm looking for?" I yell out all hopped up, to no-one. At this point my brother and my four year old son walk in asking for my car keys so he could move my car for something or other. "They're in my purse on the table." He gives me a look of horror like I just asked him to tackle the bowels of hell in nothin' but a pair of flowery flip-flops. "There's NO WAY I'm goin' through *that* mess!" he belts out. Without skipping a beat he turns to my son and says, "Never go into a woman's purse no matter what they say — you don't want that kind of trouble, let me tell ya'." I just raise my brow at him and give "the look" and shake my head with a final roll of the eyes. If there were a panel of judges I would have gotten a 9.5 for that.

Giving up on all the junk crammed into my Junk Medicine Cabinet and bleeding, I tried to grab a piece of toilet paper to wrap around my finger but someone left the empty cardboard roller on there. I put my hand in the tissue box and that's empty too. With the two males following me like a parade around the house for either some sort of bandage or paper towel going back and forth that I'm too busy to get the keys, I finally just grab a napkin and tape it on with some scotch tape from the junk drawer.

After this catastrophe I get the keys out of Junk Purse for them after having to dig through barrettes, loose coins, a matchbox car, crumbled up tissues, half a package of M&M's which apparently didn't stay closed all the way, a camera, the other Barbie shoe, a sewing kit, and ...yeah.....a rubber band!. Remember the rubber band? So I take the rubber band over to the junk drawer where I left the colored pencils and band them up. Now I still have that Kohl's receipt so I head up to the Junk Closet to see if I can locate the shirt I wanted to bring back.

After working up a sweat trying to move aside all the stuff crammed in there I saw the jacket I couldn't find last October and in the pocket low and behold was a Scooby doo band-aid. So I grab the shirt I was looking for, put the band-aid on and went to throw out the napkin and scotch tape MacGyver concoction and saw someone had thrown out the last nub of staples that can't fit into the stapler when you refill it with a fresh row. So I pick it up and put it in the bottom of the junk drawer in the event there are no staples left and we desperately needed one in an emergency.

It was a whole day of one thing leading to another in this ping pong game of looking for things in my junk drawer, closet, purse, bathroom cabinets, and don't even get me started on the bedside table drawer and the computer table. As my grandmother affectionately says, "I was goin' like a house on fire all day!" I finally sat down when my son comes in and starts sneezing. "Mommie, can I have a tissue?" "There's one in my purse — go get it." I say to him. He gives me this wide-eyed look like one Opie would give Andy Griffith and says, "Nah ah, I don't need THAT kind of trouble!"

~ BATTLE OF THE TAG SALES ~

I recently participated in the mother of all sales: The Town-wide Tag sale. Every house in the whole town had a table on their lawns with all the crap they've acquired all year. I have a girlfriend that lives in a development with her two sons and she said I could bring some of my stuff over and set up a table next to hers. Little did I know that was the beginning of a war that would be a nail biting fight to the bitter end.

Since my friend's family recently had just moved to this quaint little village they had a good-sized amount of items in storage they wanted to purge. Her two boys decided they were going to run the show. They were allowed to keep the money from anything they sold, their mother told them. Like cartoon characters their eye balls popped out with huge dollar signs blazoned upon them. Thoughts of new Wii games danced in their heads as they hocked everything they could like E-bay was having a going out of business sale. They kept running into the house and grabbing more stuff and eventually the front yard turned into a weekend bazaar stocking window blinds, kitchen appliances, toys, holiday décor, and their mothers jewelry (that I'm not so sure she actually knew about).

They had a sporting goods section with skis, skateboards, hockey equipment — they even had a boat motor going for $200. "You need a bed?" they would shout at cars going by, "We've got a queen, a couple twins, and I might be able to get you a deal on a King size!" I stood dumbfounded as I noticed that they would grab the attention of everyone walking by. "What can I interest you in today?" they would chime in like cherubs. "We have sheets, carpets and dishes in our Home Goods section," one would say. "How about some toys for your grandchildren — we have everything from a singing potty chair to Barbies and Tonka trucks — don't forget Christmas is coming and they still have the tags on them!" I literally couldn't believe it. Someone was looking for art work and they panicked since they had nothing to offer and ran back in the house. Five minutes later the younger one, Matthew, reappeared with several penciled stick figure drawings on loose leaf paper and put $12 price tags on them and shouted, "Original drawings here signed by the artist himself." I peeked over to see "Matthew" scribbled along the bottom. When they started a ladies shoe department of thirty pairs of heels I shook my head and mumbled, "Walmart's gonna be pissed!"

I didn't really think much about all this until I realized I wasn't selling anything and they had a stack of twenties in their little fists. By the time people got to the end of the row to my table they were all broke, having dumped all their cash on "those cute little boys." "How much you selling your children's books for?" asked Tommy, the nonchalant 8-year-old with a sly plan. "Three for a dollar," I replied. He went back and cut their prices selling theirs five for a dollar. I suddenly found myself trying to "up my game." I decided to re-fold my children's clothing nicer and created a lovely baby boy lumber jack ensemble of a flannel shirt tucked inside Osh Kosh B'Gosh overalls, and baby work boots. I created stylish looks for that active little girl tying a cute scarf around a pink jumper and completing the look with clogs and a headband. I wondered aloud where I had put my hangers to display my new fashions when, Gordy, the second-grader that could sell you a pair of shoes off your own feet, said, "Need a hanger? I'll sell you one of mine for $1." "That's it!" I thought, "This is WAR!" I grumbled, heading to my car, and pulled out stacks of magazines. "Free magazines at this booth today!" I shouted to passers-by giving the pint sized wheelin' n' dealin' wanna-be's my trade-mark smirk. That's when they pulled out the big guns that no adult can resist — that's right — a lemonade stand! Batting their eyelashes at me in veiled innocence they chimed, "Did we mention we were child models?" Damn! Burned by Parent magazine cover-boys! I grew desperate and started yelling like a Carnie at a sideshow booth, "Get your CD's here, people, we've got it all — Books, DVD's, video games. Need a new coffee maker? Step right up, I'm your gal!" Well, that's all I needed to do. Out came the industrial potato peeler. "Got an army to feed — this baby will peel 30 pounds of potatoes in under a minute — brand new — never used!" they screamed just glaring at me. Never saw that one comin'. Seriously?! That monster could not only peel a truckload of potatoes but looked like it could do ten loads of laundry, mix cement, and replace your man in the boudoir. I just couldn't compete with that thing.

I gave it one last shot and offered free Avon perfume samples with every purchase. They started walking around on stilts and playing the accordion for tips! All they needed was some cookies and it would have been a tag sale with dinner and a show! I was being muscled-out by a couple of four foot tall grifters in Sponge Bob shirts. What a racket they had goin' on.

~ "I'M A WATER PISTOL PACKIN' MOMMA" ~

When was the last time you had a good old fashioned spontaneous water fight out on the front lawn? Everyone has some sort of water device -- be it the sprinkler, a water balloon, your average small squirt gun, those long plastic syringe type thingy's from the dollar store, a simple hose & sprayer to your major soakers that could pass for Rambo's weapon of choice. Recently I was invited to climb into this child's world of water play and had a "blast". Well….it was more like they dunked water on me when I wasn't lookin' and I just HAD to get them back.

It was an aqua-rific battle to the death … or until somebody went runnin' off cryin', that is. My children and their friends got together for an all out Water War running around the yard like they were cuckoo bananas or lit on grandpa's cough medicine. These 1st graders weren't messin' around either - they actually had "rules" to this splashy sport of theirs. Their main # 1 rule was that nobody was allowed to squirt anyone else while they were in the process of refilling their water gun in the baby pool. Everybody had to share this plastic Walmart special to dunk their water gun and re-load so they respected that. There was an honor code that was understood -- you simply don't get your loved one when their guard is down trying to re-load. These were sophisticated kids.

Then there was some rule about not squirting in the face but I didn't adhere to that one so well. Hey – this was payback for all the yogurt I've scraped off the couch cushions in the last year alone. Besides, they look so damn cute when they're all soaked like little lost puppies in the rain. I know, I know…. Bad mommy! By the time we were done you'd think we were just rescued from the Titanic or went through a car wash but without the car. Bathing suits were saggin', hair was plastered to their faces, and the lawn was a muddy swam.

My little guy's weapon of choice, being his fingers were just too little for the water pistol trigger, was actually the water bottle; a typical Poland Spring with the sport top, enabling him to squirt over the roof with a single squeeze. My daughter musta' thought she was Annie Oakley since she was packin' two pistols with full quart capacity and the meanest snarl she could muster up in her pink ruffled "Barbie" two piece. She meant business! "Hey Mommy, remember how you forgot to pick me up from Sunday School two weeks in a row and I had to sit on the church steps for an hour listening to the priest go on and on?!" Those were the last words I heard just before a big bucket of ice cold water was dunked on me as I lay on my lounge chair. Touche! She's just lucky the hose didn't reach that far around the house as I tore after her with the sprayer on full blast and shouting, "I'm gonna get you my pretty, and your little brother too! Hee! Hee! Hee!" Unfortunately just around the corner of the house was an angry mob of pint-sized kids armed with more water balloons then I'd ever seen. While my brain was in slow motion screaming at me, "Go back! It's a trap!" they let loose their arsenal. Like a Tom and Jerry cartoon I jumped outta' my skin trying to get outta there but quick, while gettin' pelted in the back of the head. I swear I was picking colored pieces of rubber out of my hair two days later.

Out of breath, soaked, with grass stained knees I took cover to re-group. I tried calling for a back up battalion of adults but they threw me under the bus. "You're doin' fine – think of how good they'll sleep tonight," they shouted over their shoulders while sucking down cold Coronas in the shade. So I pulled a Benedict Arnold, joined forces with the half-pints and sent all those grown up's screamin' every which way trying to escape our wrath… until finally one of them held up a white T-shirt in an attempt to surrender. "Aren't you a little old for water fights, Carol?!" they angrily yelled going to find dry clothes. "Why….No…No, I'm not," I smirked.

~ "IS THERE A SNAKE IN THE BED OR ARE YOU JUST HAPPY TO SEE ME?" ~

I don't know about you, but lately the craziness of life has me shakin' my head thinkin' "I can't believe this is my life". Just in the last month the unbelievable amount of flukey weird stuff has been clearly on the rise faster than the thermometer around here.

Take for instance the fact that lately I've been catching more mice than the pied piper in my house. There seriously must be a sign up at the local rat saloon that says, "All you can eat buffet at Carol's house." The one thing I can't do is clean out the traps – that's my man's job. If he's not around I just throw the whole trap, dead mouse and all, into the trash. Then he gets mad I didn't save the trap. "That was a good trap; the spring on it was perfect and now it's a waste to buy more! Why didn't you just throw the mouse out and reset it?" he says. "Are you serious? It's only a buck for 6 traps – I don't need to be cutting corners in this area, noooooo way," I reply.

Then suddenly I wasn't getting any mice and thought they finally packed up and left but then he says, "Maybe the snake that I accidentally let loose in your house is eating them." My jaw dropped to the floor. "Snake? What snake?! And when the hell were you going to tell me?!" Apparently he caught it in the garage and let my pre-schooler play with it like it was a pet! They put it in a glass jar with a CD balanced on the top for safe keeping and forgot about it. A CD balanced on top! Like that was going to keep it securely inside! What the hell was he thinking?! I came home to find the jar turned over on the floor and thought … "hmm…that's odd."

So for the last two weeks I've been throwing back the sheets for fear of getting into bed with a little something extra slimy in it besides him. "You have to find that snake and get it out of the house," I screamed. "I did get it out" he says. "Oh, really," I say, "how did you catch it?" Get this – he actually said to me, "I opened the front door and it just slithered out into the yard," like it was a trained poodle or something! Do I really look that stupid?! Really?! Damn men!! It's that flippin' Y-chromosome of theirs!

Onward and upward in my list of flukey things. In all this rainy weather I was rushing around trying to get to work on time and dropped my son off at Grandma's when I accidentally slipped and fell into a puddle. My pants were soaked and it was too late to run home. "Ma, quick - get me some clothes I'm soppin' wet all the way through." Well, let me tell ya' – It's just super freaky havin' to go a whole day wearin' you mother's underwear. Just skeeves ya' out the whole day and you hope to God you don't have a car accident. I'd be half dead going into an operation frantically yelling, "These granny panties aren't mine – I'm wearing my mother's underwear!" They'd probably throw me out. "Somebody call the psych ward – we gotta real twisted one here!" they'd say.

Let's see – what else is on my horror show menu of oddities... Almost burnt the house down last week. Apparently dish towels aren't meant to be baked in the broiler. How it got there I have no idea but it definitely was not "dinner material" – hahahahaha. It did add a slightly different flavor to the chicken that was baking in there at the time. "What's for dinner, Mom?" "Burnt dish towel chicken almandine," I snorted back. It basically improved the taste considering my culinary skills aren't top notch.

Rounding out my list was my computer blowing up. One of those odd things you don't see everyday – like a car on fire in the Holland Tunnel. The funny part – like there's a funny part – was that my boss had just gotten done telling me that I've been late in meeting my deadline for three weeks straight. (Hey – YOU try being funny on demand in 800 words or less each week in a timely manner) So of course I panicked late Sunday night a minute before deadline when the thing just bursts into flames. If that isn't a sign from God telling me he doesn't like my column this week I don't know what is. I don't think my boss believed me either. It does sound suspiciously like "the dog ate my homework".

So I'm waiting to see what other horrible little things are lurking around the corner ready to jump out at me…like a flat tire and no spare….spilling coffee on your crotch… just barely makin' to the toilet when you have the runs only to discover there's no toilet paper…eating what you thought was a chocolate chip but it was really a mouse turd. Yup…my life is definitely a joke that needs to be thrown back in like a small fish on opening day.

~ THE MOTEL 6 FOR RODENTS ~

Spring has been threatening us to arrive all winter and has finally done so. It is a time that, yes, brings pleasure to most (except allergy sufferers perhaps) but it also is a time for taking stock of any household damages and repairs needed. This is where I take assessment of how my little cottage withstood the elements and rodents through the season. This year it was Rodents 3, Carol 0. Living out in the woods has its benefits enjoying the wildlife around you but sometimes it can be a human vs. animal battle reminiscence of Bill Murray and the rodent in "Caddyshack". As I recall it didn't end well for Murray's character.

Through out the last few months we've been the home of rabbits, skunks, squirrels, mice, spiders and a snake. They apparently thought my abode looked pretty cozy for the winter and hunkered down. Cleaning out the garage was more like going through Wild Kingdom except I wasn't in a car. Apparently the snake that lives in my garage hibernated all winter and broke our roommate agreement regarding the section of keeping the mouse population down. Mickey & Minnie Mouse opened up a saloon in a corner of the garage amongst some boxes. They musta' put on one helluva variety act for half of the Pipe Piper's drunken rats it looked like.

By the lovely odor permeating my yard I noticed my shed became the Motel 6 of the Skunk Species. They had a party for sure and invited a few thousand of their closest rabbit friends over apparently. I got a feeling this spring is gonna be bringing some funky lookin' black n' white striped rabbits around the place.

Whenever I pull down the long gravel driveway there's a few dozen rabbits and a couple of skunks having a meeting or something and I practically run over a couple of them as they scatter. They always glare at me like I interrupted something important. "Whups, this meeting of the Easter Egg Distribution Department has come to an end due to the rude human driving through our conference room once again!" The kids will yell from the back seat, "Mommy, look out you almost killed the Easter Bunny!" and then lecture me on how I almost destroyed the upcoming Holiday for all children through-out the world.

We did have one casualty amongst the squirrel's nut gathering brigade this year, however. It was a freak accident I believe with the poor fellow getting too obsessive with his nut storage capacity. Kinda' like watching one of those "Hoarder" TV Shows gone awry with the inhabitant getting trapped under their mounds of crap. Walking around the side of the house I looked at the gutter drain spout that runs from the roof down the corner of the house to the ground and runs off into the flower beds. About waist high up I noticed a hole the size of a golf ball in the middle of the pipe and it had a squirrel tail sticking out of it…. and it ain't movin'. So, of course, I had to find a stick and poke it. Nope. That is one ex-squirrel. It is no more. Now the kids have run up and want to know what I'm doing of course and I lie and say that the little fellow is sleeping and not to wake him up.

Checking out the end of the drain pipe he stuffed it so full with nuts that he could only get in from the hole three feet up; must not have been able to turn around and get back out, so he died upside down with his tail in the air… consumed by his own gluttony. What a way to go. It's definitely somethin' you don't see every day – a dead squirrel butt hanging out of the side of your house.

Well, at least it wasn't a shut out then: Rodents 3, Carol 1. I yell out the screen door to the rest of them, "That's right, there's been a casualty amongst the squirrel clan, so watch ya' selves or I'll be servin' up some roast rabbit for Easter Sunday, boys!" I swear I heard a snicker followed by a "Talk to the paw, be-yatch", but I couldn't be sure.

~ DEATH BY POWDERED SUGAR ~

So I went to a friend's funeral last weekend. Boy, everyone's been dropping dead lately. Geez, even the dog died last week. Poor thing was older than dirt and just a rack of bones so it was her time…. the dog — not my friend. I'm sure I'm gonna catch hell for writing a humor column about death but somebody needs to point out the craziness of it all.

People die in such strange ways; like the guy that robbed a supermarket by hitting the cashier over the head with a watermelon. He grabbed the cash, ran out the door, and got flattened by a produce truck carrying watermelon. I can't tell you how many people die on the toilet bowl each year. What a way to go — with your pants down on the crapper. Isadora Duncan is another quirky death. For all you young-un's, she was a famous dancer in the 1920's who just went on and on about her favorite silk scarf. Well it eventually choked her to death when it was flapping out the car window and got wound up in the tire spokes and dragged her down the street before decapitating her. I bet scarf sales dropped dramatically *that* week. Wouldn't it be funny if a unicyclist got run over by a bicycle? Or a circus tight rope walker that tripped on the sidewalk and died of an infection from the stubbed toe? One strange one was when the Recreation Department lifeguards in New Orleans celebrated their first drowning-free season ever and threw themselves a party. When the party ended one of them was dead at the bottom of the pool.

You don't ever want to go to a funeral with me because I get very anxious and can't help but break out into uncontrollable nervous laughter. So basically I'm the one at the back of the wake with a bad case of the giggles with everyone thinking I'm an insensitive slob. When I was a kid and found my sister's pet rabbit dead in the cage I had to go tell her and got so worked up laughing about it I couldn't stop. She thought I was trying to tell a joke or something and started laughing right along with me until the both of us were in tears and rolling on the floor laughing until I was finally able to blurt out "Your rabbit died!" She went off screaming to my mother that I was cruel and probably killed it.

Everyone reacts differently. My brother tends to get frustrated and ornery. At a funeral a few years back he sat impatiently in his car in a long procession waiting for the casket to be put into the hearse. "For cryin' out loud, put the damn thing in there and let's go already," he angrily yelled, beeping the horn. Mortified, I just looked at him and said slowly, "My Lord! That's our grandfather, not a sack of potatoes!" Apparently he wasn't the only one at that funeral with odd behavior — my grandmother, newly widowed, took out her grief on an unsuspecting bottle of bourbon at the reception and did the cha-cha on the dance floor with men half her age. Hmmmmmm….. maybe his demise wasn't quite the accident we were lead to believe …

Of all the funerals I've gone to none can top that of poor "Old Man Jack" as the neighborhood kids called him. He lived with his zillion year old mother, who was a horrible shrew, until one day he went out hunting. He was an avid hunter that probably ate half of the county's deer population over the years. It was no wonder they found him in the field dead with hoof prints all over him. Some doe's husband got even is what I think. They figured Old Man Jack and the deer got into a bit of a quarrel and the deer won. His last request was that he be buried with his favorite stuffed deer head which really made for a rather screwed up casket with the horns and all. What a sight! When they were carrying the casket out one of the pall bearers tripped, the casket went hurdling down the front steps at remarkable speed, popped open and the deer head flew out and landed at his mother's feet. She screamed holy terror going down the street with her walker at the top notch speed of a snail. You can't blame me for laughing at *that* funeral.

When I die I'm sure it'll be by accidentally inhaling the powered sugar off a donut and choking to death on it. I want to be laid out in the casket in my filthy bathrobe, slippers, the TV remote, a Labatts in one hand and a chicken wing in the other and wearing a Buffalo Bills hat. I figured since it's for all eternity I should be comfortable.

~ CHAPTER THREE ~

'TIS THE SEASON....

Most everyone has some rather fond memories, or maybe some rather odd memories that center around various holidays or different seasons and mine is no exception. Straight out of a Hollywood spoof flick are some interesting moments and observations that deserve noting as I take you through the seasons of Fall, Winter, Spring and Summer in Carol World.

Maybe you can sympathize with me ....

~ HALLOWEEN: MORE TRICKS THAN TREATS ~

Ah… Halloween. That time of year when you can get away with getting gobs of candy and you say to hell with the dentist. Even the strictest, "no sugar allowed" parent isn't cruel enough to let their child miss out on this time honored childhood favorite. 'Course they're probably the ones shoving apples into everybody's bags. Spoil sports! The one time of year you can get away with eating candy (oops.. can't forget Mr. Easter Bunny) and somebody has to ruin it with something healthy. Ugh. At least they don't shove cans of creamed corn in the bag — which brings up another area: candy corn. I'm sorry but "candy" and "corn" do not belong in the same sentence and they are horrid little pieces of candy that children just immediately pass off to grandma or throw into the garbage. It's pretty bad when a kid won't eat raw sugar. How that company has survived all these years I have no idea. Name one kid that likes that stuff and he's the one that gets pelted with it by other kids in the back of the school bus.

I fondly remember all the homemade costumes me and my siblings have worn over the years. There were four of us and so one year I decided to talk them into going as the "Fruit of the Loom" fruit characters (apple, grapes, etc). The rest of them backed out at the last minute and I had purple papier-mâché balls that just hung down off of strings that just got odd stares. The grapes, remember? What? I thought it would be a hit. The next year I went as a Captain Crunch cereal box but had to lie down in the back of the station wagon to fit in the car. In the country you have to drive to houses that are a mile apart and it was the worst costume to try and maneuver in and out of the wagon! Ugh! It was terrible!

Then one year my father got into the creative spirit and made a life size giraffe out of steel, wire mesh, papier-mâché, and PVC tubing for the neck. My poor sister and her friend, wearing yellow dyed long underwear for the legs, struggled under the weight of the 200lb thing at the school party. My father, rushing from work to make the event, got pulled over and the cop made him walk a line touching his nose when he tried to explain that he was going to miss the giraffe. Of course it didn't help that me and my girlfriend were dressed like hookers in the car which made the cop think he was not only drunk but a pimp as well.

Halloween is different in various stages of life. As a child you experience it by going door to door dressed in a costume nobody sees because your parents cover it up with your coat — I hated that! As a teenager you dress up as the scariest thing you can and go door to door with eggs and toilet paper wreaking havoc on all the teachers that ruined your lives. In your 20's gals dress up in skimpy costumes that would give their mother's heart attacks to impress college boys that stand around a keg making terrible puns about "tricks vs. treats". In your 30's you struggle with putting on "cute" outfits on your little ones, freeze your butt off, then stay up half the night eating their stash when they pass out from the sugar high. In your 40's you are hoping the cops don't knock on the door with your teenager holding a can of shaving cream and sporting what is hopefully fake blood. In your 50's you finally get to stay home, shell out $50 of candy to 500 strangers and "oooh" and "ahhh" over kids that cry/wet their pants and dodge eggs from teens. 60's? You don't even bother putting on the porch light and just go buy YOURSELF a big bag of candy and say to hell with the holiday. Then in the nursing home you get candy as bingo winnings and angrily complain that they don't sell candy corn anymore...

I can't even begin to describe the hell my 5 year old son has put me through since he began talking at the age of 2 years old. You see, "Halloween" is his Christmas. It's his favorite time of the year and all he wants to do is drag it out all year long. The day after Halloween is over he starts asking me when Halloween is again. By Thanksgiving he's grumbling that he doesn't like turkey and wants to know why we are carving up a perfectly good pumpkin into a pie instead of a jack-o-lantern. At Christmas when he is done opening a mound of toys, that I'll be paying off till summer, I'll ask him if he was happy Santa brought him all that he wanted and he'll say kinda' sulking, "Yeah.... I guess... but it's still not as good as Howaween." When January arrives and it's his birthday he insists on having a Halloween Birthday Party. The first year it caught me off guard and I couldn't find one Halloween plate, tablecloth or decoration in the snows of winter. So this year I smartened up and stocked up on all the Halloween decorations in preparation for this January's sad puppy dog eyes begging me for a "Pin the bolts on Frankenstein" game. Watch – this will be the year he decides he wants nothing but

Abe Lincoln decorations for his birthday.

At first I figured his obsession was candy based and that was his main goal – to get gobs of sugar without fear of parental persecution. So I thought I had him all figured out but then Easter rolled around and with the onset of the Easter Bunny and getting a whole basket of sugar delights I thought for sure he'd say that now Easter was his favorite holiday. Apparently it wasn't the candy that was the big draw. He didn't really get into the chocolate bunnies, jelly beans, and such and just turned his nose up dismissing the whole thing like a pile of turnips.

Every summer I had to hear on a weekly basis constant whining which he got down to an art form. "But, M-O-M-M-Y, how much wonger to Howaweeeeeeeeeeeen????" We'd be having a fun Fourth of July BBQ playing in the pool in the sweltering heat and he'd start in with it. I just shook my head and wondered how much therapy would cost me because there's obviously something wrong with this kid.

As soon as the first nip of cool air arrives in the first week of September he's just about whipped in to a frenzy asking me on a DAILY basis when he can get his Halloween costume. "Sweety, they're not even out on the shelves yet," I try to dissuade him to no avail. By this time he's insisted we decorate the entire house inside and out with a ton of Halloween decorations that will be there from the first day of school in September till I put my foot down mid December and insist on Christmas decorations.

By the time October hits he's frothing at the mouth like a rabid raccoon. He announces he's got a list of possible costumes but hasn't narrowed it down to which one he wants yet. I find this particularly amusing since he doesn't know how to read or write yet. So he hands over his "list" which is a bunch of strange stick figure drawings splattered in various colors. "See, dis one has big scawee teef cuz it's a shark, and dis one has wots of blood on his mowf cuz it's a zombie doctor – but it's just fake – it's not weal. Then dis one has a cwazy alwien with a spaceship coming out of his bewee button." God, when he grows up and can pronounce his "L's" and says, "belly" the right way I am gonna cry for the days when he was cute as hell saying "bewee".

Well, I suppose I only have myself to blame for passing on my "freak" gene to my offspring. It's amazing to see your children pull the same nutball stuff you did as a child. All those childhood years that my mother said to me "Watch – when you have kids of your own you're gonna get it back ten-fold" apparently has come true. So as I cook dinner thinking about Halloween and all its enticing allure I decide if you can't beat 'em, join 'em. I pop in some vampire teeth, throw on a cape, and serve him his dinner of spaghetti and meatballs, and in my best Count Dracula voice say, "Here's your guts and eyeballs to feast on, my little monster," and he bursts out into laughter and says, "You forgot the spiders!"

~ TIME TO GIT YER PIE ON! ~

If someone from another country asked you what Thanksgiving means to you, what would you say? Everyone has a different feeling about that day. To some people it would be about the historical premise of the Native Americans and the Pilgrims sitting down to a huge feast, a time of peace, coming together in gratitude for the bountiful harvest. To some people it's just another day out of the year and "Ding" the pot pie's ready to eat in front of the tube, amidst rambunctious screams at the quarterback.

Some of my friends would say what matters most to them is the Macy's Thanksgiving Day Parade and how they've been going to it each year. Some of the male folk say it's all about getting up at 5am and freezing their tails off in a tree-stand waiting for an animal to slaughter with their shotgun. [Grunt] "I am Testosterone Man — hear me roar!" On the flip side the women chime in that Thanksgiving is a cooking technicality they suffer through just to get to Black Friday and the thrill of the shopping hunt. "Get out of my way lady, that last sweater on sale is mine, I have my charge card, and I know how to use it, so step off!"

My father would say it's about bringing home strangers to our family turkey dinner each year. People that have no place to go because their own family can't even stand to be around them, wind up at our table. Inevitably forks clatter onto the plate and looks of "them's fightin' words" are shot at one another as blows are thrown and the bourbon starts flowing. Good times! Good times!

To me it's about all about the pie. In my family I am the "Pie Master" and all bow to me in homage of the great pies bestowed upon them every year. Each Thanksgiving morning I wake up singing the pie song that Andie McDowell sang in the Movie "Michael" with John Travolta playing the Archangel Michael. "Pie, Pie, me oh my! Apple, Pumpkin, Mince and Black Bottom. I'll come to your house every day if you got 'em. Pie, Pie, I love Pie!" Starts the day off on the right foot for me, I'd say. Last year my older brother decided to make the pie in an obvious sibling rivalry bake off to the finish. He sniffed his nose in the air at my crumb topping and sprinkling of raisins in the mix for some added flavoring. He opted more for a pastry covering but when I noted his apples were still crunchy and not enough flour was added so it was runny he just flippantly said, "I made it that way on purpose!" I just rolled my eyes..

Everyone has their favorites of course. Apple and pumpkin are a given on this day but my cousin always wants a chocolate cream, my brother-in-law wants strawberry rhubarb and says mine is better than his mothers, [insert my internal evil pie villain's bwa-ha-ha snicker here]. If I don't make a blueberry one with cream cheese swirls in it one family member gets bent out of shape. God help me if the day passes without a lemon meringue for Grandma and of course little Jimmy who's really starting to look a bit ape-ish throws a fit for Banana cream. Some nutballs always insist I make a mince meat pie which just sounds so gross to me — the word "meat" and "pie" just sound so wrong together. Kinda like "Sheppard's Pie" — you get all excited thinking you're gonna get a plate full of sugary sweetness baked by some cute Sheppardess in clogs and you wind up with mashed potatoes and meat made by Hungry Jack. Ugh!

Did you ever see the movie, *Waitress*? Super movie, tragic result, the writer/director struggled her whole life to become famous, makes this incredible movie and just before it hits big at the Tri-beca film festival is murdered. The film was about a waitress that has a gift for making pies and she names them very strange names depending on what's going on in her life. "I hate Monday's" Pie, or "I don't want to have Earl's baby" Pie, and then my favorite, "I don't get paid enough" Pie. If I took to naming my pies I could probably think of some doosies like "If I step in dog poop one more time I could scream" Pie (that one would most likely be chocolate in nature) or how about "My grandparents went to Disney and all I got was this lousy pie" Pie. That one would be made of gold to reflect the enormous overcharging you endure at this rat-themed greedy park. If I baked a pie yesterday it would have been named the "Bloody Mary" pie after the woman that ran a red light, almost killing me and then had the nerve to flip ME the bird. If I had my handy dandy "Circus Clown Pie" I would have thrown that sky-high whipped confection in her face. Ba-dum-bum! Ching!

So there you have it. Thanksgiving summed up in a few words: Pilgrims and Native Americans, Macy's parade, Black Friday, the NFL, deer hunting, turkey dinner, the family arguments, the bourbon and Pie. Pie seems to be the topping on the whole shebang, smoothing out the wrinkles and making people happy. Can't say it makes the dog happy though: this year he's been giving me these sad eyes and I just KNOW he's thinking, "When the hell are you going to make me a Milk Bone Pie?!"

~ FALLING FOR THE FESTIVAL ~

Somehow, somewhere, long ago people decided that they needed some sort of an excuse to eat a ton of food and therefore they invented "the Festival" to honor their favorite food in the Harvest time of the year. What a great way to spend a crisp fall afternoon. Since the winter is just too damn cold and nobody wants to come out of hibernation people probably figured the fall would be the last hoorah to chow down and party before hunkering down like a bear. We have festivals that celebrate just about every kind of food possible. Everything from typical Harvest themes of Pumpkin Festivals and Apple Festivals to Rib Fests, Pickle Fests and Garlic Fests. Let's not forget the Oktoberfest which celebrates heavily endowed women that look like the Swiss Miss with a frosty beer in one hand and a wiener schnitzel in the other.

A good many of these festivals celebrate normal foods and fun accompanied with hay rides, pumpkins, candy apples, and the petting of farm animals. But there are some odd food festivals that just go beyond all reason and begs the question, "What is wrong with these people?" In the "Battle of the Oranges" in Italy you get pummeled by oranges (NOT the way I prefer to get my vitamin C). In the "Night of the Radishes" in Mexico they make huge floats made entirely out of carved radishes. I never liked radishes. Let's not forget England with their annual cheese rolling festival. They roll a huge round hunk of cheese the size of my steering wheel down a hill for some odd reason. I don't think I want a slice of cheese on my wheat thin that has grass sticking out the top. Lastly it's not a party without mentioning Spain's Annual Tomato Festival whereby they load up a bunch of trucks with over 100 tons of tomatoes that they dump over 40,000 people that attend this massive food fight. At the end of that day I wouldn't be saying, "I wish I had a V-8".

One of my favorite memories of my childhood, was going to the Vermont Bread n' Butter Festival with my little 7 year old cousin Matthew, siblings and parents on a road trip up to see the hippy cousins in some Woodstock-like field on a rainy, soggy day. I was hopin' for some pie with all that bread and butter but there wasn't any bread or butter – they lied. It wasn't that kinda festival. It was some weird artistic hippy gathering with small stages of actors playing out political satire sketches. To get out of the rain we stumbled into the back of a tent filled with a Russian theatre group putting on make-up, changing costumes, drinking vodka and smokin' up the weed. Everyone just turned and looked at my shocked Brady Bunch Family. My father just shoves us all back outta the tent, "Whooops, pardon us, wrong tent, we're going now." A short time later we were all sitting on the ground, front row watching some Moses-type skit that was very odd, when suddenly one of the actors from the tent appears on stage in a long sheppard's tunic shouting, "My name is Isaiah and I saya to you …(he pauses like he was gonna puke but then tries to start again… "I say my name is Isaiah and I saya to YOU I am ----" and with that he stumbles and falls flat on his face! Matthew jumps to his feet and yells, "DRUNK". That got him a round of laughter from the crowd. For the rest of the weekend the little guy hammed it up repeating, "My name is Isaiah and I saya to you, I'm Drunk!" before keeling over to the rest of us laughing hysterically every time. I was mostly ornery because I didn't get any Bread n' Butter for Pete's sake.

I think the next festival I simply must go to is the "Road Kill Cook-Off Festival" in Virginia. I'm not sure I'd eat any of the food they'd be serving however. Apparently all entries must have as their main ingredient any animal commonly found dead on the side of the road – groundhog, opossum, deer, rabbit, cat, squirrel, snake, dog, goat etc.. They do state, however, that the animal can be killed, gutted and cleaned prior to the cook off, but that special allowance will be made for fresh road kill occurring en route to the cook-off. I wonder how many people swerved on purpose to hit poor Bambi just for that extra point. Unfortunately the judges will deduct points for every chipped tooth resulting from gravel not removed from the road kill. The judges are picked for their cast-iron stomachs and have sworn under oath to have no vegetarian tendencies. Yeah, this is one food competition I will never want to judge.

So wherever your taste buds drag you to this Fall Festival Season, make sure you have plenty of napkins and it doesn't have tire tracks on it.

~ LOOK OUT, BAMBI, IT'S HUNTING SEASON! ~

As the season starts to jump closer to Thanksgiving, the animals start having nervous breakdowns. This brings up that timeless Elmer Fudd polishing his rifle while Bugs and Daffy are arguing in a panicked frenzy, "It's Rabbit Season", "Duck Season", "Rabbit Season", "Duck Season", over and over again. Poor things start to lose it over the mounting stress of it all and just start throwing themselves into on-coming traffic. Why else do so many deer get hit?! It's because their suicidal, I'm tellin' ya.

My mother won't let my father hunt on their ten acres though. She actually feeds the deer out in the field with a big trough of feed! "Here you go, Bambi, go tell your friends," she coos. Since she forbids my father to hunt on our land he goes across the street to the neighbor's property. She even makes him use a bow and arrow to give the deer a fighting chance. I'm sure anytime now she'll be standing across the street in her bathrobe with a big sign saying, "All deer welcome across the street!"

Wasn't always like that. Originally my family were city folk and moved up here to enjoy the country and kill all living things in it, like any gun toting local. During the 1970's when the economy was much like it is now, (hah!) good old Dad had to forage around for deer to feed his hungry brood. I can't tell you the amount of God awful venison I ate as a child. My mother would try to slip one by us now and then, "What's for dinner, ma?" "Hamburgers." One sniff and you knew. "You're lying! These are venison burgers," we would cry with endless tears. If you've never eaten deer meat thank your lucky stars because it tastes like the sole of a shoe! There's just no amount of ketchup that's gonna help it either. Throw every condiment you can at it and maybe you might be able to stomach it but don't bet on it. Just when you think you got it down you throw up a little in your mouth. Sorry… it's just so nasty. I'd rather eat snake meat, honestly, at least that tastes like chicken.

Whose idea was it to stuff the head of a deer and stick it on the wall like it was art? Seriously, what moron sat around and said, "Hey, I think I'll just chop the head off this carcass and stick it on the cave wall and admire my fine taste in décor?" What qualifies this as remotely fashionable I have no idea. I once dated a man that actually had over ten heads in his house — some of them with the front hooves! Every room of the house, wherever you looked, there were those bug eyes staring out in lifeless horror. It really gave me the creeps — I broke up with him solely because I was afraid one day MY head would wind up on the wall with a plaque stating "girlfriend who couldn't accept my killing hobby."

At one point my parents thought it would be a good idea to raise and kill our own meat to save money and to know it came from a good home I suppose. There I was with my siblings, loving our new pet cow we named, "Big Boy" and even trained it to come when we called it. We'd whistle and yell "Big Boy" and on cue you'd hear, "padump, padump, padump" and he'd run up from the backwoods to cuddle up to us. Then one day he didn't come. Our little childish hearts were stricken with fear over what became of our beloved "Big Boy" and we pleaded at the dinner table for Dad to go out on a search party lest he be in some sort of peril out there. After listening to tearful pleas and his own mounting guilt my father blurted out in exasperation, "You want to know where Big Boy is? Well, you're eatin' em! He's on your plate." We were shocked like someone just smacked us in the face with a shovel and electrocuted us. So it was back to the venison from then on. (Sigh) I wonder if that's why we're all vegetarians now.

~ BEWARE OF BLACK FRIDAY! ~

Black Friday — the day that heralds in the holiday shopping season the day after Thanksgiving. Everybody but the poor retailer has off and they have to deal with the fact that we're all miserable from the extra ten pounds we put on the day before and our intense desire to save a buck. Black Friday was a term that supposedly originated in Philadelphia in the 1960's. The media have used it to refer to the beginning of the period in which retailers go from being in the red to being in the black (i.e. turning a profit).

I personally think it got started because all the mall employees would dress in black and cringe with dread at the mere mention of the day. To them it's like going to their own funeral! Just put yourself in their shoes — they have to deal with endless lines of cranky bloodthirsty women wanting that extra 15% off. You wouldn't catch a man getting up at 4 a.m. to go to a flippin' mall. Nooooooo..... It's become a rite of passage from mothers to daughters like an annual pilgrimage paying homage to the mall with its promises of bargains galore.

Tis the season to be jolly they say, but not on Black Friday. On Black Friday you will mow down any woman trying to get the last medium-sized sweater on sale and then rip it out of her hands all in the name of "giving" for the holidays. Its cut throat out there just trying to get a parking spot. God help you if you have to unload some packages in your car — you'll get some other lady following you to your spot and cursing you out when she realizes you're not leaving and she has to circle the mall another few hundred times.

My Aunt Marie comes completely prepared as if she's running a marathon or something. She sleeps in her blue velour sweat suit so she can just jump out of bed at the crack of dawn ready to go. She leaves her coat in the car so she doesn't have to carry it when she gets too hot, and wears the best pair of flat shoes that will go the distance like a Rocky sequel. She scoffs at others struggling with their bulky purses, taking pride in her fanny pack stocked with about fifteen credit cards and a diet coke to stay hydrated. She's seasoned enough to take a recyclable shopping bag because she's learned the plastic ones rip too easily and dig into your arm. She has made shopping a sport and laughs as she outlasts the others that foolishly wore heels, heavy coats and (God Forbid) actually brought their kids along!!! "Stupid, Woman!" she laughs to herself watching the poor schleps trying to calm their whiney screaming kids.

She can go hours without going to the restroom or stopping to eat because she packs protein bars and wears astronaut diapers — the woman is hard core I tell ya'. Like a shopping superhero she packs extra coupons for the scatterbrains that have lost theirs, and can talk any cashier into giving her the extra senior citizen discount on top of the already reduced clearance item with a store coupon. This woman can walk away with a brand new pair of Ann Taylor slacks for $2.50 — I've seen it with my own eyes. She can outlast that stupid pink energizer bunny — no problem.

And the stores! They're all getting ready like it's the Kentucky Derby or something! I can almost hear a crazed psychotic announcer calling the race! "Okay folks, here's the Black Friday bell....And they're off!!! We've got Walmart in the lead with a pair of cell phones on sale but coming up quick on their heels is Circuit City with a bottom basement IPod that can't be beat…..oooh, looks like Target just sold out on the hottest toy in town and they're down for the count… lastly it's Toys-R-Us bringing up the rear with only a GI Joe left to spare and …WHOA! Out of nowhere Barbie's are flying off the shelf at Kohl's with an unprecedented 50% off coupon by a nose!! And its Kohl's winning by a nose at this Black Friday event, folks, there you have it!"

Yep, it's cuckoo bananas all right but, hey, what else you gonna do the day after Thanksgiving? Grab your fanny packs, ladies, starting time is 4 a.m. …we're off!!!

~ THE CHRISTMAS THAT WENT AWRY... ~

Christmas. This single word can evoke many emotions ranging from joy to nausea. With me it's a lot of both. The holidays are fun but somehow they can be a little nerve-wracking wouldn't you say?

My family still has those huge 1970's outdoor lights. These strands of light bulbs are nothing but a box of 8-track tapes to me. Oh, and don't even think of throwing them out. "They're still good, don't throw out that strand." "Dad! There's only two working lights on the whole thing and they don't make the replacement bulbs anymore." "I can't see getting rid of it. Maybe they'll make them again." So then I roll my eyes. Ever notice how everyone is a professional on how to hang lights but nobody wants to actually get on the ladder with the staple gun to do it? So all of us feel it's our duty to direct my father while he's on the ladder. "No, honey, it's got to go higher on the left side of Rudolph's nose." "Dad, if you put it that way all the red bulbs will be clumped together and it's gonna look stupid." "Honey, that last part just fell back down." At about this point my father wants to staple gun our foreheads and starts muttering that in about two damn minutes we can do it our damn selves. At which point we all mumble, "What the hell is his problem?" and go back inside.

The tree. Ahhh, the tree. What a tradition that is, huh? Whose idea was it to bring the forest into the house anyways? With my family we would always chop down our own tree in the wilderness. After three hours of arguing about which one to get we would begin the ordeal of chopping it down and almost taking a leg off in the process. After a few years of that my father came home with a tree that he got from the gas station. The gas fumes from the tree were so bad we had to have all the windows open to keep from passing out. The poor thing lost all its needles in two days and by Christmas looked like a hat rack. I really wanted to take out the .22 and shoot it to put it out of its misery.

The decorating of said tree was always a blast. When we were small the tree consisted of hand-made pasty oatmeal ornaments that looked like the art class rejects along with those garland strands of chained construction paper. For years I thought it was a family tradition to decorate the tree on Christmas Eve. As an adult I realized the rest of the world would call this procrastination. When we were kids we all argued about who got more ornaments to put on and how unfair my parents were. As teenagers my mother would threaten us to put the ornaments on. "Damn it, if you kids don't start decorating this tree I'm bringing everything back to the mall!"

Who thought of the idea of a fat man with a limited wardrobe, a binging "cookie and milk" eating disorder, and a fetish for having kids sit on his lap swearing they were "good"? Think about this — doesn't anybody think that a strange person breaking into your house late at night via the friggin' chimney for God's sake, isn't the slightest bit scary and peculiar? And we actually tell our kids this load of crap?!! When I was a kid I was so confused — one minute you're told not to talk to strangers yet some guy was sneaking into the house once a year in his long johns! What's wrong with this picture? Is it any wonder that kids cry on Santa's lap at the mall?

I think this is going be the year that my nieces finally realize there's no Santa. Last year we just squeaked it by them. They were starting to get suspicious but then a stroke of luck — on the way home from Midnight Mass we saw a guy walking down the road in a Santa suit so we stopped to say hello and show the girls that he really was real since he was caught coming out of a house. Let me tell you — that Santa was so lit on bourbon he could've juiced up the sleigh with about a thousand volts. He leans in the car window with some wet, sticky candy canes he probably just dug out of the bottom of his boot and hiccupped what was supposed to be, I imagine, a "Ho! Ho!" but came out like a "Hup! Burp! Pfpt. Sputter" So the girls are squealing out, "Santa! Where's your sleigh?" "Oh, uh, it's back in the woods there with my eight reindeer." With that, like perfect timing, we hear a gun shot. "Whup, make that seven reindeer. Looks like Mrs. Claus is making venison burgers tonight." What the..? Their eyes were stuck open all night long like ping-pong balls on acid. My God! Another innocent holiday shot to hell. This year I think instead of cookies for Santa they'll be leaving him vegetarian cookbooks and brochures for AA.

You know it's not really Christmas until your Uncle Frank starts hittin' the booze. Things start getting pretty lively after that, the language gets very colorful, and the women start swearing the men are ruining Christmas. By this time, to change the subject, my mother starts in on me: "You meet anybody yet?" "Wouldn't hurt you to wear a little make-up once in awhile." "Have you gained weight?" "So I guess you're not going to have anybody to kiss on New Year's Eve again this year, huh?" Then just when you think it can't get any worse you hear, "Where's everybody sleeping?" knowing full well you're gonna be forced to give up your bed for somebody. Oy. Happy flippin' holidays to me.

~ BAD GIFT GIVERS...
HO, HO, FLIPPIN' HO! ~

Don't ya hate it when someone in your family is a bad "gift giver"? For years and years you suffer through the most bizarre, unusual, ugly, and downright insulting gifts imaginable. The first few years you tried to make a fuss and put on your "company face" with a half-assed smile. "Wow, that's neat... I didn't even know that nose-picking devices had been invented ... ooh... it even has a booger collection feature... wow... guess you can find anything at that fancy gadgity store in the mall."

Over the years you may have even gotten pretty good at faking it with phrases, like "Thank you, it's very interesting." That one's a favorite of mine. Chances are if I've used the "interesting" phrase on you Christmas morning you can be sure your gift was at my yard sale that following spring. Although, when you get something like a toilet snake for your birthday from your husband you're pretty much past the interesting phrase and have entered, the "Really?!" phase of your relationship accompanied with a snarl and a heart stopping glare. Then again you could be one of those well-organized and efficient people that think everything should have a purpose and be useful and would like a toilet snake. "Great, a toilet snake, we really needed to give the crapper a good cleaning; what a thoughtful gift," your wife jubilantly chimes in. If this is the case the magic is gone, baby, give it up.

I had a string of ex-boyfriends that were either the worst gift givers in the world or they were trying to get me to break up with them. When your man shows up to your house on Christmas well after the festivities are over blaring "Happy Easter, Baby" and stinkin' of Jack you know you picked a winner. In my case he was also very proud to be surprising me with a set of lovely white fluffy towels that said "Holiday Inn" on them. He would continually cheap out and buy me gifts at tag sales for a buck and then lie about it and say he found it in this cute Vermont country store. "It was sooo expensive, Carol, so be careful with it."

I even get bad gifts from companies. In my stay-at-home mommy years, with an infant and a toddler, I'd get free products from local plastic surgeons along with a warning that now I need to fix my boobs since breast feeding has wrecked them. Right in the mailbox next to them would be a "gift" of free breath freshener from the local singles dating network saying "Hey, if your marriage is on the rocks, why not get back into dating for fun?" What a way to support the bonds of marriage during this holiest of seasons.

Now, listen up all you men, when Christmas rolls around and you've been with your lady for five plus years there better be a ring under that tree or she's gonna run outta there crying in a major meltdown of nuclear proportions. There's nothing worse than when your girlfriends are hinting that he may just pop the question, getting all excited about it, then he shows up with nothing but a Tweety bird t-shirt with a matching Sylvester the cat sweatshirt. That happened to me and like an idiot I thought, "This couldn't possibly be my gift — I don't wear cartoon t-shirts... oh, maybe the ring is in the pocket to throw me off.." So I frantically searched the pockets, looked in the discarded gift wrap, turned it inside and out a few dozen times, THEN burst into tears. There's nothing worse than a man that doesn't realize that after five years, enough is enough and flippin' propose already! Needless to say that relationship didn't even last till New Years.

For Christmas this year I think I just want an economy-sized gallon jug of Xanax, an uninterrupted night's sleep, and elves that will clean my dishes while I sleep. Cheers.

~ SLEIGH-RIDING SHOULD BE AN OLYMPIC SPORT ~

Sleigh-riding is the most fun anyone can have in the middle of winter — and it's free! The best sleds I've used with my children are those round plastic saucers that go shooting down the hill at 100mph. Back in the day, however, sleds consisted of several slats of wood nailed upon two red runners with a rudimentary steering bar. As a child my siblings and I turned sleigh-riding into a bloody sport of fists-and-will on the most hellish cliffs in history.

This hill was the steepest, bumpiest, rugged piece of earth covered with sprouting trees, razor-sharp prickers, boulders the size of bulldozers and to add insult to injury at the bottom of the hill was a barbed wire fence surrounding what you hoped was a "frozen" pond at the time. After a day of sleigh-riding getting slashed by all of these natural elements it rendered us unrecognizable by our mother. In short, this was the sleigh-riding hill from hell and we loved it with sick pleasure and with no regard for our humanly existence.

Now, at the time we had two sleds in a nature that could be called, "rusting, warped, pieces of crap held together with hope and spit" that would terrify the hell out of any adult. At first we behaved as normal kids did and took turns riding slowly in a safe path past the obstacles at a cautious speed. Eventually though boredom and creativity got the best of us and knocked about eight lives off us that winter. It was the year that Howard Cosell and "Crash-up Derbies" were in favor with our clan. My older brother did a great impression of Howard's blood-pumping, on-the-edge-of-your-seat, play-by-bloody-play, kind of voice accelerated to insane childish decibels. This coincided well with "Crash-up Derbies" which was a popular past-time of stock cars smashing the hell out of each other on national television. We combined both elements and put it into experimental practice in the form of sleigh-riding – which we no longer referred to as "sleigh-riding". Sleigh-riding was for well-behaved sane children. On a winter's morning we would just yell, "Hey! Let's go play Crash-up Derbies, guys!" I can imagine what my mother thought.

We divided up into teams of two kids each on two sleds. The point of the sport would be to beat the living daylights out of the rival passengers on their sled while hurling down this God-forsaken hill at 100mph crashing sleds all the way down. My parent's probably wondered why the shiny Red Rider Specials we got at Christmas looked like tree bark with tin foil brackets by January.

The siblings that were steering had the objective to smash into the other team's sled and try to send them off course into the woods. The objective of the back passengers was to knock the crap out of the other team's back passenger, jump over to their sled, knock the driver off and gain possession of the rival sled. Remember the barbed wire fence? If by some slim chance we actually made it to the bottom, someone would yell "FENCE!" and rather quickly we would have to lay down on the sled making it under the fence and onto the frozen pond. This was the biggest thrill as decapitation was always a possibility as well as the thin ice, drowning with a sled anchor, along with sibling that was a lousy driver. We were absolute pros in powder blue snowsuits.

To give you a slight taste of one episode you'll have to imagine this in the very interesting speech of Howard Cosell as told by my brother: "This is HOWard Cosell, comin' to you LIVE at the TOP of the hill! We're AT the Starting gate, Ladies, n' Gentlemen, n' what a fine day it is for Crash Up Derbies. Who will take home the Crown of Victory? Will it be the Undefeated Blue Knight team or the Red Baron team — and Incredible Bunch of Losers. On Your Marks, Get Set, Go-o-o-o!! They're neck n' neck as they go barrelin' down! Ooohhh! The Red Baron team crashes into the Blue Knights! A quick jab to the ribs!! This is a kill all game to the end! It's a bloody battle rounding the first corner — whoaa! A jab to the left! A right hook to the jaw! They both fall off the back of their sleds sending the Red Baron alone across the finish line and under the barbed wire fence with his head intact onto the rarely frozen pond to victory!!"

So there you have it — a simple past-time of gliding down a hill turned into a warped and twisted violent sport by lunatic third graders. That's what it was like growing up with my brood. How my parents actually survived us I have no idea. I often think of stuff like that as I'm insisting my children sit properly on the sleds, holding tightly to the handles, on a very small slope without any trees or boulders. What an "un-fun" Mommy I am.

~ NEW YEAR'S RESOLUTIONS, FIGGIE PUDDING AND THERAPY, OH MY! ~

Ahh…the New Year is here, and like newborn babies we're filled with determination, hope, and anticipation for glorious things to come. We all have our list of resolutions of ways to improve ourselves that we swear we're really going to keep this year. Time to try out that new hairstyle, lose those few extra pounds, get that great raise at work, and find the love of your life….or so you think. It's actually a therapist's dream come true.

January starts out with the best of intentions with a huge boost of energy to make good on all those promises, but like a slowly deflating tire, it just sorta' peters out. That new haircut goes horribly askew and friends will look at various bald spots on your head and ask, "Holy smokes, what happened?! Are you dying or something?" The few pounds you wanted to lose typically results in some size-two woman barking out aerobics commands like a true Nazi: "C'mon, ladies, work off that Figgie pudding or your butt will start to *look* like Figgie pudding!" This usually lands one into therapy to hammer out pathetic self-esteem issues that had to be scraped off the gym floor like stale gum.

Around the end of the month, the credit cards roll in from the holidays and the depression sets in like a bad round of swine flu with an "oink oink" here and an "oink oink" there. They say the most depressing day of the year is January 24th. Apparently it's the one day of the year that massive amounts of suicides happen. It's also my ex-husband's birthday…hmmm…that explains an awful lot. So at this point you not only have those few extra pounds on your mind but the stress from the credit card debt for little Suzy's $100 American Doll she just *had* to have. Once again the therapist makes out like a bandit.

Typically, this time is when people get laid off from work as well. The big-wig bosses really wanted to do it prior to the holidays but didn't want to be total boneheads so they waited till the holidays were over and blamed it on the new budget. Another resolution bites the dust. No climbing the corporate ladder this year. That whole new wonderful feeling of moving up in the world is replaced by a feeling in your stomach that thumps like sneakers in the dryer. I hate how they always decide to fire you at the end of the day after they've gotten a full day's worth of work out of you. How crappy is that? Studies show they typically do it mid-week instead of Fridays because the suicide rate is lower that way. Who does these ridiculous studies? If you get fired on a Wednesday or a Friday it doesn't matter, because your first stop is the bar since, obviously, the weekend just started earlier for you than your former co-workers. Hopefully they don't have the unemployment office next to any bridges or the coast guard would be awfully busy pulling in soggy jumpers like marshmallows in a cup of hot cocoa. Missed opportunity for the therapists right there — they dropped the body…I mean "ball" on those cases.

Oh, and new love? Let's just not even go there. If you're like me, your ego is still bruised from not kissing anyone at midnight on New Year's Eve and soon the evil eye of Valentine's Day will be breathing down your neck. That's a whole other column right there. Never was there such a dastardly anti-singles day aimed at rubbing one's love-less life back into one's face. But yet we trudge on and join Match.com, Cupid.com, E-Harmony, Singles-R-Us and every other ridiculous dating site out there in the hopes of finding that one person among millions that will complete us. It's a lovely thought and you actually believe it and fork over the $24.95. Unfortunately, the attractive people in their ads are not anything close to the real people that subscribe to these services. Frightening mutants that are twenty years older than you, with the personalities of tree fungus, that just e-mail you perverse things and/or nekkid pictures of their thangs – that's who are on those sites.

So what's the moral of this story? The kick in the head that sets off the light bulb and makes it all okay? The, "Oh… I get it" factor? Say to hell with New Year's resolutions and be happy with who you are and the life you have and everything else will just fall into place like brushing your teeth each day. Now that's a good New Year's resolution.

I would have made a great therapist…I'd make a killing if I set up a desk on the Newburgh-Beacon bridge talking all those jumpers off the ledge and saving lives…. No.. wait.. cancel that – my mother would come for a visit at my bridge desk and she has a tendency to make people want to jump so I'd lose a lotta clients that way.

~ THE WINTER BLAH, LAUNDROMAT FIGHT, ATTACK OF THE OWL KINGDOM STORY ~

Lately I've had that commercial on my mind where the old lady fell and she yells into her life alert chain, "Help, I've fallen and I can't get up!" It kinda sums up my life right about now except mine's more of a "Help, I'm miserable and I don't know why!"

It could be that I just can't figure out why I have 11 black socks and none of them match; God, that really chaps my hide. The bills rolling in from all the Christmas overspending is a big contributor to the winter blahs, but that ain't it. It could be because no matter how much I try I can't fix this stupid slinky. Why do they even make them? Immediately out of the package it's inevitable that the kid will somehow get it crossed and on the dump heap it goes. Losing the extra weight I put on over the holidays is definitely adding to the huge heap of brain laundry renting space in my head.

Speaking of laundry — I bet it's because when I went to the Laundromat this week some woman took my still wet clothes out of the dryer (that had just stopped) to put her own in. I was scrounging in my purse for another quarter to put it in for another fifteen minutes and she just whips my stuff out! So we got into it and I took out my Colt .45 and pistol-whipped her until she begged for forgiveness.

Just kidding — I only thought it. But I did give her a nasty glare and call her rude. A verbal war of words ensued to the delight of many a bored laundry patron thrilled at the impromptu realty TV show happening live in front of them for a Sunday afternoon viewing pleasure.

Perhaps it could be because I keep getting my socks wet from the puddles of snow on the floor my kids track in. No matter how much you try to avoid it, inevitably you're heading to the sock drawer for another pair. Not that it matters because you're feet are already frozen because the house is so flippin' cold and never seems to heat up. Winter equals rock salt, shoveling mounds of snow, your socks scrunched down to your toes inside your boot, scraping ice off the windshield, getting into a cold car, snot running outta the kid's nose and having to walk a constipated dog in the middle of a snowstorm.

Hmm — you know, I think it's because I'm a little creeped out about the bird kingdom lately since I believe they've declared war against me as of late. Wherever I go they keep flying into me like I'm in a Hitchcock film. Three times in a week I've been attacked by various feathered friends — and I'm a huge bird fan! It's apparently a bad omen, unless they crap on you — that apparently is good luck; go figure. I did have a bird crap on me once. I yelled back at it, "Go ahead, everybody else does!"

So here I am drivin' around the mountain on my way home, minding my own business and whistling "she'll be comin' round the mountain" when *bam*, this huge flippin' owl flies right into my side window. Holy Smokes! I couldn't believe it. "Well, now, you don't see that every day!" I shouted. It was huge and hit the window so hard it moved the car and I swerved.

I got out to check on him. He was stunned. I was stunned. I mean most people have never seen an owl, let alone hit one. Maybe he needs glasses like Mr. Magoo. He was probably thinking, "Damn, that was one big fuckin' mouse I just hit!"

A few days later in the middle of Christmas dinner, I'm sitting in front of a large window when a beautiful red cardinal hits the window right behind me and falls down dead. Right in front of me! So now, I'm starting to get a little jumpy because somethin' is messed up with that! It can't be a coincidence, right?!

Suddenly my mother enters the room and asked about the bang. I look around the room at all the cardinal statues, cardinal paintings, cardinal salt and pepper shakers, wood saws with cardinals painted on them, cardinal dish towels, quilted cardinal wall hangings, cardinal pottery and the rest of the cardinal shrine …and then at my mother…. who's wearing a cardinal sweater with matching cardinal earrings and have to tell her a cardinal just died outside her window on flippin' Christmas morning! Let's just say it didn't make for good dinner conversation.

But wait — there's more. What are the chances of actually getting hit by yet *another* owl in one's lifetime, let alone in the same week? Yup, it happened again! On the way home from New Year's Eve dinner another owl came flying right at me like some twisted game of chicken I didn't even know I was playin'! I actually screamed and ducked down as it went splat right on the windshield and then up over the roof.

"What the hell is up with these birds?" I screamed. If the owl population suddenly drops in this area and they put up signs of my blue momma min-van with red circles and lines through it I want everyone to know they started it! As far as those 500 birds falling out of the sky in the mid-west, I had nothing to do with it, I swear! I've never even been to those states!

No wonder I've been little squirrelly lately. Help, I've fallen and I can't get up! I'm being attacked by birds which are obviously giving me the heebie-jeebies bad omen vibe which is leading to crazed Laundromat Gone Wild episodes, snow in my boot, messed up slinkys, cardinal shrines, a fat ass and 11 wet black socks…. Yup. It's gonna be a great year!!!

~ "I GOT MARRIED BY A GROUNDHOG!" ~

Have you ever noticed that February 2nd is right smack dab in the heart of winter? It was a date that basically helped the Punxsutawney, Pennsylvania immigrant German farmers in the 1800's ration out their hay and feed. If they had half of their hay left to last the animals by that date they'd be okay to last out the winter and if not were screwed — unless it was an early Spring.

Of course the next step was a way to figure out how to predict if they were going to have an early spring. They remembered that the Europeans found using a hedgehog useful in this endeavor, but being there were more ground hogs overrunning the place on this side of the ocean, the farmers figured it was a good substitute. Besides "Hedge Hog day" just doesn't have that special zing.

A bunch of good old boys, sick of the snow and winter, were probably sitting around a bonfire in the woods drinking from Grandpa's secret batch of cough medicine percolating in the 'still' behind them when a ground hog suddenly popped up out of its hole, cast a shadow and ran back in. "Did you just see that there woodchuck thing, Zeke?" "Yup, I done did there Bobby Mack ….can't be good -- gotta be a bad omen."

Drunk on whiskey (and since comic books, gun clubs, and fishing contests weren't invented yet) they, like most men, went back and forth for the next three hours about why would "Phil" (of course they had to name it, along with his wife Phyllis) did such a thing like run back inside like that. "It musta' saw all the snow and said, 'Hell no, I ain't going out there' which means we gonna have real skinny cows come April." "Is that right, there, Zeke? You think our, <hiccup> our little buddy Phil here says spring is way the hell off?"

"Yup"

"Well, then, there's only one thing to do then — have a party."

"Well now, that seems like a good idea there, Bobby Mack, but what to call it? Woodchuck Weather Report Day?"

"Nah — too formal.

How about "Hedgehog Predictions-R-Us?"

"Nah — too long. Let's just call it 'groundhog's day' plain and simple."

The local paper, *"The Punxatawney Spirit"* decided it sounded like a good idea too, especially since the last exciting thing that happened was old pop Miller's sow had a pig with a weird tail. So they announced a big shindig was gonna be thrown in honor of Punxsutawney Phil each year, stating boldly on February 2, 1886, "Today is groundhog day, and up to the time of going to press, the beast has not seen his shadow."

So, basically, they all got together and partied down after grabbing the poor rodent out of its hole and dragging it up to Gobbler's Knob all in a desperate attempt to put the shovels away. They warmed up on a few corn squeezins', hacked up a few ice blocks into ground hog effigy like statues and probably ate pie. It's just not a celebration without some pie — and maybe some light explosives in the sky, although in 1886 they didn't have fireworks yet so they probably shot off their bow and arrows of flaming dried cow poop on a stick.

I read they actually give Phil his own special "groundhog punch" (probably corn squeezins') each February 2, which has helped him survive over 100 years. Well that and a hearty diet, and what with his wife Phyllis as his backbone, the thing has held up all these years.

His most notable year on record was during prohibition when the local news reported that Phil "threatened to impose sixty weeks of winter on the community if he wasn't allowed to drink". Guess he got a little ornery when it was last call for the groundhog punch. Maybe Phil's own celebrity status started getting to him and, like Charlie Sheen, was put into rehab. Phyllis probably had it up to here with him. I heard that in 1995, Phil appeared on Oprah with the Governor and said he was much clearer now in his predictions and proclaimed a glorious spring for all, while jumping up and down on her couch.

I just read that in recent years a bunch of people that attended Punxsutawney, PA's yearly February 2 celebration wanted to get married right then and there. So believe it not the locals, probably still two sheets to the wind like their ancestors, said 'Why not?' Yup, that's right; you can get married in Punxsutawney with Phil as the officiate.

That would be an interesting icebreaker at a party, "Mark and I were married by a member of the woodchuck family, Punxsutawney Phil, very reputable as a meteorologist. He even made our wedding frame himself that he carved from a branch from Gobbler's Knob."

I wouldn't be able to hold it in and inevitably I'd stick my foot in my mouth and say something like, "And did Donald Duck baptize your daughter?"

Well, after all this, hell broke loose and many other groups of people decided they were getting cabin fever and wanted their own celebratory traditions too. Like the Irish decided March 17 was a good date to have a pint and name it after their brother, Patrick, who was a real saint. The Hispanics finally jumped on the bandwagon with "Cinco de Mayo" and lots of tequila. They named it "Cinco de Mayo" which means the fifth day of May to help them remember which day they were gonna celebrate — probably the fault of the tequila. Then all the men from every culture banded together and cried out for their own mid-winter holiday-like-festival with its own statue and snazzy name.

"We shall have our own holiday in the middle of winter, with food and beer galore and it shall be called, "The Superbowl!" And it all started with the groundhog —who probably is saying to himself: "What the hell does a groundhog have to do to get some sleep around here?!"

~ "DON'T EVER SPRAY THE BLARNEY STONE WITH SANITIZER!" ~

Obviously St. Paddy's day is a big ta-do there in Ireland since Saint Patrick was a legend in their Christian heritage; although through the years it's rampantly become a non-secular day of celebration. Everyone wears the color green, dons a shamrock perhaps, and say's things like, "Kiss me, I'm Irish". It's a day that's filled with the consumption of some fine ale, a hearty meal of corned beef n' cabbage, and the hope of a leprechaun leaving a pot of gold at your door.

Whenever I think of St. Patrick's day and all things Irish, I think of my parent's last vacation to Ireland. They went on a Seniors Trip with their cousins, two other couples, all about the same late 60's retired age. The six of them are referred to in our extended family as "The Six Pack". They can easily be described as "Seniors Gone Wild". Their perspective is that they raised their children and grandchildren; worked their middle class jobs to the bone, and saved their whole lives -- so now they're gonna have some fun, ***dammit***, even if it kills 'em. I'm writing a movie about them because these baby boomers have really had some wild adventures. Have mercy! They are such a great example of 'fun at 65' that I'm actually looking forward to my future sixties.

They partied their way through Ireland for the feast of St. Paddy's day a couple years ago. Apparently they got thrown off the Guiness tour for being a little too tipsy and rowdy. "Whoop! Whoop! Go Grandma/Go Grandpa!" Having sampled all that the lovely brewery could offer from ale to stout these giggling, gafaw-ing adorable shlepps got a bit too carried away for the other seniors on this tour. So they had to have a "Seniors Time Out" and had to wait on the bus for the rest of the well behaved members of "the Happy Seniors Sunshine Group" to complete their day's tour. As they described it, one got laughing about their mishap with their hearing aid, then add in a couple of pints of the summer brew, and then it goes viral with all of them hysterically laughing until one of them had to grab an inhaler and another their Nitro. Baby boomers on Guiness and heart meds… swell.

For starters what happened earlier in the day was cousin Barbara's hearing aid battery died in one ear. So the new battery wouldn't stick in properly in the unit, nor in her ear, and somehow crazy glue entered the equation with two of the men trying to get in on the act. End Result? In the vast stony hills of Ireland along a dirt road in a little village, three of them were stuck together and trying to make their bickering way with baby steps to a shop in search of some sort of solvent. Apparently two of the men had their fingers glued to her ear along with the hearing aid at a failed attempt to help her with said device. I'm sure the locals got a kick out of the sight of a woman walking down the road with the hands of two men glued to her ear.

Eventually a shop owner took pity, and a bottle of nail polish remover enabled them all to be detached. Since they don't have a Rite-Aid in every goat pasture there, they were very lucky they didn't have to spend the whole trip glued together. Silly Americans!

By the end of the day it was amazing they weren't thrown out of Ireland altogether as their little mishaps just got grew into major catastrophes that involved a major country icon, the "Blarney Stone". As the saying goes, it's good luck to kiss the blarney stone. It's a large boulder that's built into the rock wall of Blarney Castle that lies on a cliff overlooking the raging waters below. Legend has it a Queen, having been saved from drowning by the castle's owner, put a magical spell on the stone that whoever kissed it would receive the powers of persuasion. Well, it apparently didn't work for my mother, for she did NOT receive the power of persuasion to get herself out of trouble for desecrating this historical stone, getting yelled at by the caretakers of said treasured icon.

I guess she had heard the locals go up there drunk at night and piss on the thing and laugh it up thinking of all the tourists that kiss it. So she decided to pull out a bottle of sanitizer and a paper towel and give that Blarney Stone a good wipe down before kissing it for good luck, which is …apparently from all the wild gestures and brogue cursing… you're not allowed to do that. I guess it's bad luck to spray the Blarney Stone with sanitizer. Another place in Ireland they are now forever banned from. You may ask what kind of person has a bottle of cleaning fluid and a roll of paper towels in her purse; mothers that's who. Mothers have everything in their purse like Mary Poppins pulling out a hat rack.

So, now, forevermore, whenever I think of Ireland, St. Patrick's Day, and all that jazz, I laugh thinking about how this Six Pack of fun loving Baby Boomers represented America. Happy St. Patrick's Day!

~ APRIL FOOL'S BABY ~

Yup, believe it or not, today is my birthday. A humor columnist born on April Fool's Day — Ha! That's a joke in itself. I wonder if God was sitting there that day and said, "Let's see, all the little darlings I'm cookin' up to be born today will be very funny." Hmmm…makes you wonder if all the scary whack-nuts out there were born on Halloween. Or if you were born on Black Friday you might have an obsessive compulsion to hit every sale in town, or if it was Labor Day weekend you'd vaguely resemble Jerry Lewis. People born on Groundhogs Day eventually having careers as weatherman would be funny too, wouldn't it? At any rate, I have to say that being born on April Fool's day really does explain a lot. I always seem to get myself into such odd predicaments that I feel like a Court Jester on a rollercoaster with Lucille Ball.

Unfortunately though, since everyone knows it's your birthday, you become the butt of every stupid attempt to get your goat. At this point in my life, if I actually had a goat I'd offer it up as a sacrifice just to be left out of this crazed ritual of being fooled on this day. I'm particularly jumpy waiting for just about every idiot to jump out of the bushes, drop a water balloon on my head, throw grape Kool-Aid on me in the shower (you'll be purple for two days), sew the legs of my underwear shut so I fall on my naked butt, tell me they overheard my boss saying he was gonna fire me, or have some scary clown throw a pie in my face.

The best one was one year my friends were designated drivers at my birthday bash and drove me home. When they got me home, they parked the car on my front lawn, put me in the driver's seat, and somehow put a white picket fence on the grill of the car and road kill on the hood. I woke up in the morning horrified at the sight, to my cell phone ringing with a fake cop telling me I had to come down to the station to answer a few questions about a dead dog and some old lady's picket fence. Let's see, it's been several years and although they all said I'd be laughing about that someday I just checked my funny bone and it still says that wasn't funny at all. Nope, not laughing yet, guys.

So far the day has already started off with a bang this year. Tripped and fell down the stairs this morning, which means sitting here typing this with a sore bomba - not the least bit of fun right now. The hem on my pants broke loose when I got to work, and I contemplated if the stapler or the plastic brown packing tape would be the better choice. The tape won out since the stapler would look too obvious. Unfortunately now when I walk around the office there's this plastic swishing sound that makes me sound like I'm wearing a diaper. Goes right along with the fact that I lost the back of my earring and so I had to use a pencil eraser to stick on it. I'm becoming the MacGyver of fashion mishaps. Heloise's Household tips ain't got nothin' on me today.

If that doesn't put the icing on my birthday cake, I also came in to work to find that a little mouse has eaten all my pre-Easter candy in my drawer and crapped everywhere. (Pre-Easter candy is the candy you buy for your kids for Easter but after two days you've eaten all ten bags and then have to quickly rush out and see if there's anything left on the shelves so as not to break their little hearts in two that the Easter Bunny blew it again this year.) I noticed that little ol' Mickey Mouse didn't even bother with the diet fiber bars. Smart-ass mouse; I'm waiting for it to jump up and yell "April Fool's" but don't see that happenin' anytime soon. If it did I'd be rich with a talking mouse. It'd be a bonus if it could do vaudeville routine with a little cane and top hat. I think I've been watching too many Tom & Jerry cartoons.

So how will the rest of the day go, I wonder. Will I get an exploding birthday cake? Will I accidentally tuck the back of my skirt into my pantyhose and walk half-way down Main Street to the tune of several snickers? I could win the lottery perhaps, but then I'd think it was a joke and throw out the ticket and it will wind up in a landfill in Guam where it will be eaten by another mouse that doesn't have Easter Candy like its rich cousin in America. So, yeah, typical April Fool's birthday in Carol Land. Hope yours was better.

~ BURN, BABY, BURN! ~

I was wondering the other day about all the skin problems that start to arise when the weather gets warmer. Things like getting poison ivy covering half your body, skin poisoning from laying out in the sun too long, burning yourself on the grill etc... All horrible evils that I abhor. Wouldn't you know it - faster than you can say voodoo doll, the universe decided to answer my random pondering in a real Charlie Daniel's fiddle playin' "devil went down to Georgia" type thing.

The weekend started out innocently enough trying to get some yard work done when low and behold I got some poison ivy. I tried not to panic and remember the time I looked like a leper about to lose a finger, as every inch of me was swollen and blotchy from climbing a tree covered in pretty shiny vines. Getting poison ivy at the very start of what was supposed to be a great sunny weekend filled with festivals and celebrations was not going to deter me. I was going to have a good time no matter what.

Saturday rolls around and my whole family is gathering for my niece's birthday party and a big BBQ cook out was planned complete with a rented inflatable bouncy house for the kids and plenty of margaritas for the adults. As soon as I get out of the car and before I get to say hello to anyone I decided to sit on my friend's motorcycle for a minute since it's been all winter since I've had the chance to do such. Just as he's saying, "Don't put your foot on the hot pipe," I did just that. Since I was wearing my new black strappy sandals I immediately knew about that hot pipe. Running or hobbling quickly in heels to their front door was not my most proudest moment as I nearly knocked the pregnant woman down as I rushed for the ice trays. I just wanted to put my whole foot in the beer cooler. "This is not good," I thought, as every nerve in my body screamed in agony.

My father chastised me the whole party saying I was showboating when I couldn't even walk on it or keep the ice off for more than twenty seconds without screaming bloody hell. Thank God there was booze and that bouncy house kept my kids bouncing all afternoon. I was still determined to enjoy myself and sat with my foot up on a bag of ice as I soaked up some rays on the deck talking to the ladies and enjoying my wine. "It's so nice to have a glass of wine since I've been on antibiotics for the last ten days from bronchitis," I say. I was happy to finally relax even if I was itching from poison ivy and my foot was now scarred for all eternity. "Better be careful in the sun, honey, I think you get a burn if you're on antibiotics," mom chimes in. Then my sister adds her two cents, "No you don't get a burn from being on antibiotics you get a rabid yeast infection; you need to take acidophilus so you don't get one." "Ass-of-phil? What the hell?" I said with a snarky look. I was stunned as the conversation became too "R" rated for this column. "Ladies, break it up, let me just have my wine and my sun, and enjoy myself. I've been a little pasty white from the winter anyways and vitamin D is good for your mood." "All right but don't call me up tonight saying you're burned from head to toe, missy," my mom warns.

So I thought about all this and how the universe did indeed teach me a lesson in which skin ailment is the worst to suffer through as I called my mother on the phone. "Mother, I'll have you know I am burned from head-to-toe from sunburn that is so bad I'm pickling myself in vinegar and slathering on gobs of vitamin E syrup which hopefully doesn't flair up the poison ivy to spread further. I'm doing all of this while I'm sitting on a bag of ice and balancing the other one on my foot." She pauses for a moment and says, "Wait a minute …I know you burned your foot on the motorcycle… but why are you sitting on a bag of ice?" "Let's just say my sister was right about getting some Monistat because my Ass is on fire too!" Needless to say, I burned, baby, burned.

~ BATHING SUITS ARE NOTHIN' BUT EVIL IN SPANDEX! ~

Bathing suit shopping should be outlawed. Never have I paid such an enormous amount of money to feel this humiliated. For some reason they have the uncanny ability to squeeze, distort, and enlarge body parts making you look like a Macy's Day float. Trying them on in the lime green light of the department store dressing room can shatter even the strongest self-image, giving you nightmares of yourself starring as Shamoo, the killer whale, at Sea World. All dressing rooms should come equipped with barf bags. Never mind the fact that it's like an Olympic sport trying to get into them and breaking a sweat as you wrestle it like an insane python. Putting a bra on a rhino and squeezin' its fat ass into granny panties would be easier I think. Sorry for all the animal references — still trying to get my blood pressure back to normal after this devastating experience. Unlike the slogan for milk, it's quite obvious there's just no amount of colorful spandex that's "gonna do my body good."

I soooooooo don't believe any of those lousy chick magazines anymore either, with their stupid advice on the type of bathing suit that will flatter any frame whether you're top heavy or got junk in the trunk. Lies, lies, all lies. What you find in the mall are wretched colors with all sorts of tassels, sequins, and bows that succeed in making you look like a cheesy, washed up, Vegas show girl on crack. I'd be a shoo-in as a Carnival clown making balloon animals in some of those get-ups. Who on earth would make a bathing suit with thick horizontal brown and orange stripes? Are we beach balls for cryin' out loud? "You'll be able to find me, Susie, because I'll be the third beach ball to the left of the life guard station." We'd blend in with all the other beach balls at the shore making for a rather sick type of camouflage.

Ahh… but then by some miracle from heaven you hear trumpets and the sounds of angels as you find THE ONE. The one bathing suit that is going to solve all your spare tire problems, cottage cheese thighs, and hike your boobs up and off your stomach. But then sadly you look at the price tag and realize you paid less for your car and get a lump in your throat as you put it back on the rack with tears in your eyes. Sigh… money actually CAN make anyone look good. I sneer at those Victoria Secret models on TV. "Wouldn't look so hot without all that lipo, botox, boob implants and a million dollar bikini made of diamonds, now would ya?!"

The stress that society puts on you is terrible, isn't it? Recently I went shopping with my 6 year old daughter to try on bathing suits and *she's* even stressing about it and told me she wanted to get on my treadmill. First grade and already has body issues — poor thing! We went through dozens of Disney princess ones, ruffled butt ones, Hannah "I have no talent" Montana ones, ugly plaid ones, and neon orange ones till we finally settled on a black one which looks like we're about to attend a funeral pool party. I would have bought the neon orange one but figured people would confuse it with prison clothes — which reminds me — I think some people should get convicted of a felony for some of the suits they wear.

It is my personal opinion that no man of any shape should wear a Speedo. It's just wrong. Wrong in so many ways I wouldn't know where to start. It doesn't even matter if you're good looking — say "no" for all of humanity and revolt against it! Another rule should be that you have to qualify for a 2-piece bathing suit because someone needs to tell the size 25 woman that she can't wear a size 2 G-string for fear that the Lord will start the apocalypse on humanity as punishment for lack of judgment! I don't like looking at my own fat ass looking this horrible and just can't subject other people to the torture of havin' to look at it at the beach. It's honestly not good for the digestion. So, people, both men and women … exercise some good judgment so we can all keep our lunches down.

The worst thing bathing manufacturers do (and you don't find out about until you've bought the suit and are wearing it into a body of water) is that they can be see-through. I will never buy another white bathing suit for that reason. What were they thinking?! Of course, nobody tells you, but suddenly you notice everyone staring oddly. At first you think "Hey, maybe I'm looking better than I thought" but then some nosy kid points to you and yells, "Mommy, I can see that lady's booby nickels." That's one bathing suit that ends up in the trash almost immediately. It's reasons like this that department stores say there's no return policy on bathing suits – because they know once you figure out what's wrong with them they'll have a lawsuit on their hands. Well, after a month of searching I still can't find a decent bathing suit. What a shame because I LOVE to do laps in the pool. Guess I'll just have to build a fence and start skinny dipping.

The Ice Cream Man....

~ THE ICE CREAM MAN ~

Ice Cream makes people happy. It just does. That frozen delight in the form of cherry vanilla, mint chocolate chip, forbidden chocolate fudge, and cookies n' cream can bring a kid-like smile to anybody's face. Whether it's in a boat with a banana, whipped into a shake, or in a sugar cone with sprinkles it's sweet, cold and refreshing. So unless you're lactose intolerant or were born without taste buds, you might have belted out a round of, "Who screams for ice cream? We all scream for ice cream!"

When I think about my long history with this delectable dessert I realize the Ice Cream Man has been the one constant in my life that never let me down – a cold frozen version of Willy Wonka. Just the sound of that tinkling bell of the Ice Cream Truck coming around the corner in the streets of Jersey, just when you were in the middle of a street game of stick ball, was like a slice of heaven. All the neighborhood kids would be whipped into a frenzy running to their houses screaming "Maaaaaa,, I need money. He's gonna leave.. hurrrrrry". Frozen love on a stick on a hot summer day.

It's no wonder my first job was actually at an ice cream stand – best damn one as a matter of fact – Richard's in Montgomery, New York. Richard and his wife Charlotte were friends of my parents and gave me my first real job as a teenager. Most stands today have your typical soft serve which is child's play and a sad excuse for the art of ice cream making if you ask me. Then you're further insulted when you realize their hard ice cream is shipped in from some factory. Richard always made his own ice cream from scratch with real ingredients and his flavors were culinary masterpieces. His cackling laughter as he playfully teased his wife in the stand as he made his sweet cream was infectious. If ever there was an Ice Cream Man Richard embodied the title whole heartedly…. Well… except that he didn't have a bunch of oompa loompa's making the ice cream at night.

In college I made the big time working for Friendly's during summer break and developed the forearm of a man from all that scooping. I should have entered into a couple of arm wrestling competitions – I could have made a killin'. The uniforms left a lot to be desired though. Friendly's blue and white checkered tablecloth-like dresses with that big blue bow on the front, like we were a jar of Hellmann's mayonnaise, was definitely not in fashion…. especially when you had splotches of chocolate or peanut butter ice cream on the boobs from leaning over into the bins. By the end of the night I look like I went ten rounds with a Jim Dandy Sundae and tragically lost. I can't tell you how many comments I got at the bar after my midnight shift was over. Reeses would have been appalled.

My mother has a healthy addiction to the stuff. She was tickled pink when I would bring crates of the stuff home from work. She went through withdrawal when I moved away after college and she had to get her own – which she did – going on a major binge. They had to buy an extra freezer to hold all the ones she got on sale that were 2 for 1 and she'd buy 8 of them. When I came home from college and opened the freezer there wasn't one package of ground beef or frozen peas – it was stuffed full with every variety of ice cream humanly possible. Maybe it was empty nest syndrome or menopause or something. "When you kids went away to college I realized I didn't want to cook dinner anymore and if I damn well want ice cream for dinner every night I damn well will." I slowly backed away from the freezer not wanting to poke this bear anymore lest I get a limb chewed off by this woman formerly known as my mother.

Hands down the most fun activity to do with kids is to make homemade ice cream from scratch taking turns cranking the handle and shoveling in more rock salt and ice. When the electricity would go out in the middle of the winter, like it often did growing up in the woods, my parents would pass the time by candlelight cranking out ice cream singing old songs from the fifties. It was always the best ice cream ever creating happy family memories.

So who doesn't love ice cream? It's a cornerstone of our childhood and is the one thing that makes you feel like a kid again when it's handed to you with a napkin and a smile from the Ice Cream Man.

Author's note: In memory of Richard, for all the years of serving delicious nostalgia with a smile – you are truly Montgomery's ultimate Ice Cream Man

~ A GOOD TIME WITH EXPLOSIVES ~

It doesn't get any more "Good-old-American-Norman Rockwell-hometown-apple pie-goodness" than the Fourth of July. In every little hometown in America there's a marching band parade complete with little leaguers, bag pipers, and hay bale floats with a "Little Miss Dairy Princess" waving on top. For just about a half mile all the kids are sitting on the curb waiting to catch candy being thrown from the boy and girl scout troops walking by proudly displaying their banners. Then of course there's the local town politicians being driven in some fancy antique chitty-chitty-bang-bang car with a horn that goes "aaahhh-ooooo-gggaaa." I really try hard not to think of my taxes and sneer at them when they go by.

What would you categorize as the best part of such a day? The fact that you actually got a day off of work? The rickety home-made soap box derbies with 5 year old daredevils steering out of control? The slew of craft vendors with crocheted toilet paper covers? The roar of the music from the live bands comprised of high school kids who think they're rock stars? Or perhaps it's the great BBQ, a cold brew, and friends we haven't seen in years. Now all that is fantastic but by far the best thing about the Fourth of July is the fireworks. It just wouldn't be the Fourth of July without major amounts of explosives!

I've seen fireworks standing on a Manhattan rooftop looking at the colorful bursts above the Statue of Liberty, at the end of a Georgia country fair, and aboard a yacht anchored off of Block Island. Newport, Rhode Island has a nice display of them and the ones they shoot off the boats in Palm Beach, Florida light up the water they explode over. The worst ones were in Jersey — need I say more? The best ones I've ever seen were in Long Island when I used to live on the north shore near a firework factory. Periodically they'd do some testing of some new concoctions they were experimenting with and many a night I'd pull my lawn chair out onto the beach and watch them from the shore. I wasn't so crazy about all the loud "booms" (I can remember holding my ears and hiding my head in my mother's lap as a child when they went off – just like my kids do with me now). The shapes were cool though — yellow smiley faces, red hearts and green dollar signs. I still can't figure out how they did those!

Let's not forget that stash of fireworks your dad got illegally at some roadside tent or from the "South of the Border" in South Carolina — now that's a real pyromaniac's dream come true right there. "But it's for the kids," he laughs at his scowling wife grumbling that "he's gonna blow his arm off." Why is it that all parents give kids those "sparklers" to hold? I was scared half to death that I was going to get a spark in my eye or burn myself beyond recognition. I try to steer my kids away from them but there's always some drunk old coot trying to shove one in their hands at a party. [rolling eyes]

One year we took my father's stash of illegal fireworks and decided to start the party without him. We accidentally lit the whole bag of fireworks off from one little spark and in doing so trapped ourselves in the corner of the porch as the place lit up like a carnival ride with us screaming holy terror and making a break for the screen door. It was mom that exploded after that and dad saw a few fireworks of his own.

I used to have this next door neighbor when I lived down South that seemed to not know the Revolutionary War was over. Every Fourth of July he'd dress up in his Confederate gear looking like

Ichabod Crane and blast all sorts of old time patriotic tunes from the farm house which was practically covered in flags. He'd even set up male dummies in the yard dressed either as Union soldiers or Confederate soldiers and even had one sitting on a life-size wooden horse statue. Each year he'd invite me over for his shindig with all his funky relatives and so after years of this, I decided to go over one time. Now all that time he said he was shooting off fireworks in the back field so I wanted to check them out. His idea of fireworks was slightly different than mine however. He had about 10 cannons he was shooting off in addition to a couple dozen muskets. They were all dippin' into Grandpa's cough medicine and whooping it off blasting the hell out of those cannons. The cannon balls would make it about 150 feet to their targets which consisted of a porcelain tub, an old TV set, a toilet bowl and an outhouse. Maybe he finally renovated and got indoor plumbing and didn't need an outdoor bathroom anymore — who knows? It's hard to guess because he just had piles of junk everywhere. I did like those breaking glass sounds though and lighting off a major arsenal is not something you get to do every day.

So no matter how you celebrate this historical day of celebration, enjoy it with your loved ones… and some fireworks of course.

~ "HOT DOGS! GET 'YER HOT DAWGS, HERE!!" ~

Summer weekends are all about the BBQ and grilling up meat. Grillin' is the man's job – I keep away from that world. Anything to do with gas and flames scares the hell outta' me. I own a grill but never use it because I'm too afraid to light it. Whenever I feel like having something on the grill I have to invite someone to come over so I can force them to light it for me. I don't have a problem putting the meat on and flipping the stuff over but turning on the gas, lighting the flame, turning off the gas – well that's just a catastrophe waiting to happen in Carol land.

It stems from one instance as a child witnessing my brother light a charcoal grill. Apparently there was too much accelerant, (knowing him it was probably gasoline or homemade rocket fuel), and upon lighting that match .. well… let's just say … one "poof" later his eyebrows and bangs were no more. I like my eyebrows intact, thank you very much. But this ain't about grilling, or eyebrows or whether it's a man or woman's territory. It's about that American tradition of celebrating the summer with a good old fashioned cook-out featuring the star of the show… the "Hot Dog".

It's summertime. Hot dogs are center stage on the grill, and at picnics all across America. They're at the ballpark, roasting on sticks over camp fires, sold from carts on city streets, rolled into pigs-in-a-blanket and makes a great beanie-weenie casserole. It's not hard to find them. Whether you call it a white hot, bagel dog, hot Texas wiener, a Dodger dog, Fenway Frank, or have it Chicago style with tomatoes and onions - it hits the spot with a pickle, and a cold brew.

Some are partial to a typical sauerkraut/relish/mustard dog which is the preferred way to eat it in the north east, while chili dogs are big in the south, 'pardner. I'm sure out in California they smother it in avocado, while in Jersey they prefer it with peppers & onions in tomato sauce complete with a "fahgetabouit" aftertaste.

Now typically one doesn't want to know what's in a hot dog since its long been rumored to be of all sorts of horrid things that could kill us or once responded to the name "spot" when called. Most companies follow the "Don't ask, Don't tell" rule and it's probably best we don't know. In Germany, where they originated, they did use dog meat now and then – hence the name. Hopefully when Mr. Felman, the German immigrant who introduced them to Coney Island in 1870, didn't serve up his little Fido.

Now the National Hot Dog Council estimates that we Americans buy about 837 million packages of hot dogs and consume about 20 billion dogs a year. Hell, the 4th of July alone over 150 million are consumed. Wow, that's alotta wieners. The most expensive hot dog sold for $69 at the 2010 National Hot Dog Day. It was made by some big shot chef, of course, who piled on weird stuff like duck and caviar. Strange. If I was going to pay $69 for a hot dog it better be laced with gold. Well, since the frank is one of America's favorite summer sandwiches, it's only fitting that this dog gets its day of course. Each year on July 23rd it's National Hot Dog Day so it'd be only fitting that we raise our wieners in celebration toasting to this unique food choice.

Right about now the hamburger is saying, "What the hell? A column on grilling meat and I don't even get a mention?" It's true some things go together like ketchup & mustard, salt & pepper, peanut butter and jelly, so I suppose I should mention the hamburger. Hot dogs and hamburgers are typically the twins of 'grilled meat land' served up together to satisfy every taste. Every time I think of hamburgers I can't help but belt out, "I like mine with lettuce and tomato, a big kosher pickle and a cold draft beer..." from Jimmy Buffet's song, "Cheeseburger in Paradise". Yeah I know I said hot dogs were perfect with a big pickle and a cold draft beer, but a juicy burger with grilled onions is right up there too .... hmm.. maybe I just like stuff to go with a pickle and a beer.

But they both absolutely HAVE to be accompanied by their step-sibling – the baked beans – and there you have it - the super hero trio of the back yard BBQ. Hamburgers, Hot Dogs and Baked Beans are the stuff that makes an ordinary day of sittin' around the house into a backyard summer shindig that makes you get the camera out. Meat to the rescue!

Well, all this hot dog and hamburger talk and finally some decent weather, is making me in the mood for the stuff. Isn't it funny how a nice sunny day makes you crave a good cook out with family and friends in the backyard? Hmm.. now who can I call to come over and light my grill...?

~ ROW, ROW, ROW YOUR BOAT ~

I rowed a boat last weekend but it definitely wasn't down a gentle stream merrily, merrily, merrily. Me and a gal pal, also a single mother, decided to take our little ones on a raft adventure down the Delaware River; sort of a last hoorah of the summer before the school bell rings next week. It started out great but somehow turned into something messy that Lucy and Ethel would have gotten themselves into.

Considering my friend is a city slicker it was quiet enjoyable seeing her out of her element, and together with three kids under the age of nine it became a Larry, Curley and Moe flick. This motley crew of misfits brought to mind that old saying of being up Shit's creek without a paddle so rather than end up at the end of the river without any paddles or kids left aboard we decided to take extra's….. (paddles that is – not kids) ~smirk~. So we filled the raft with kids, coolers, and about eight oars hoping not to drown or end up lost in Pennsylvania.

Unfortunately with all those oars there wasn't much room to sit and being outnumbered by children that liked to flail about with these wooden tools it was only a matter of time before one of us got whacked and thrown overboard by an overzealous second grader. And that would be me of course… knocked backwards into the water by an oar…. which seemed to even amuse the ducks as they swarmed around me quackin' up a storm like I had a carton of saltines in my pockets just for them. Now although seeing someone in a comedy flick getting smacked in the back of the head with a boat oar and thrown overboard is hilariously funny, I assure you, in reality it ain't a real "ha ha" moment. "Thanks, guys… hope I didn't lose the car keys at the bottom of the river." I don't think they heard me since they could barely catch their breath from laughing so hard.

After about an hour we started to get the hang of the oars rowing down the river and I was feeling all Huck Finn-like happy to spending a beautiful day with my kiddidle-doo's when the river picked up a little in speed and we started getting tossed around like we were in a washing machine on spin cycle. I was compelled to belt out the theme song to Gilligan's Island which only produced puzzling looks on everyone's faces being too young to remember such a good show. After the part about the 'weather getting rough and the tiny ship was lost' those looks turned into wide eyed panic and my friend snarled, "Steer the raft Mrs. Howl or you're gonna shipwreck us all." I was appalled! "Hey, I may not be the movie star but I could pass for a Mary Anne! I certainly ain't no Mrs. Howl - that's just plain mean!"

One thing for sure is that was the rockiest river I've ever seen in my life. Not like I've seen a lot of rivers but this one seemed to have a ton of rocks peppered all over the place like a mine field. If there was a rock in that river we either hit it or got hung up on it and had to get out and push… reminded me of my car. After my girlfriend lost her shoe and we watched it float away I was appointed the one to get us off the rocks which only made me want to yell, "Iceberg dead ahead" but they didn't get that reference either. I made a mental note to throw out all those horrid Sponge Bob Square Pants DVD's and rent some Julie Andrews musicals.

Not long after that the thunder started and so did the rain. I think about the time one of the kids said, "Do you hear a hissing sound? Is the raft leaking air?" Can you believe it? Either the last rock ripped us a hole or somehow out of over a hundred rafts they had piled sky high we picked one with a rip in it. With a couple miles yet to go and praying that the rubber raft would hold together and protect us from the lightning bolts, all I could do was yell, "Paddle faster kids! Stroke! Stroke! Stroke!" Course at that point I felt like I was gonna HAVE a stroke. … especially when we hit the eel traps that were set in the middle of the river with big warning signs --- I thought for sure if we didn't get electrocuted by the lightning the eels would get us for sure. I thought of all the eel sushi I ate in the past and promised I'd give it up we made it out alive.

When all was said and done and we were back in the car all wet and pooped, I was surprised to hear they all wanted to do it again next year saying it was the best fun ever. Although the kids insisted they did all the work to the incredulous laughter of the adults, my sore muscles begged to differ on that one the next day. Maybe next year we'll rent a motor boat instead.

~ CHAPTER FOUR ~

THE FAMILY THAT STAYS TOGETHER GET'S AWFULLY SQUIRELLY

Who doesn't have a few nuts in their family? We all do…. Some of us have more nuts than others perhaps though… Some of the names of my family members have been changed to protect the guilty … others I left their real names in there, 'cause they deserve a little bit of poking. Other parts of my family history I have no excuse for …..

~ MY GRANDPA WAS A MUSKRAT! ~

Ever wonder where you came from? Unless you're a pure 100% pedigree Italian, Russian, Chinese etc…moving to this neck of the woods recently, chances are you're a mixed breed of various cultures. America is often referred to as the melting pot but at this point I think we're all a bunch of waxy candles some of whom are lit most of the time.

Well, for years I've been threatening to look up my genealogy and apparently some of my ancestors were lit most of the time too. I turned up the information of my native ancestry and apparently my great-great-grandmother was a Misogi Apache. She was a slave that was owned, I also discovered, by President Zachary Taylor, our 12th President, and she was also his mistress. Apparently these are the loins from which I stem from. Not crazy about poor grandma being a slave and a mistress, but I must admit, at least she went big time with a president and probably got some good perks from it all. I was rather proud of this presidential pedigree heritage at least until I delved into the life of Zachary Taylor and came upon some unbelievable gossip. From a few various sources on the internet (all hail the internet) a few oddities about him were listed. Don't know who came up with it and what their sources were but it pretty much does sound quite characteristic of my relatives.

Apparently Zachary's election to the highest office in the land was, naturally, a fluke. In an effort to make something of himself and earn the respect of his friends, he half-heartedly declared his candidacy for president in the 1849 election. They completely made fun of him and painted slogan signs that read, "A muskrat in every pot." I guess somehow they nicknamed him "Muskrat Head" when he was born and he's always hated it with a passion. The mere mention of the word or sight of a muskrat sent him into a rage.

His opponent, Samuel Gates, was an enormously popular Governor who was running unopposed and considered a shoe-in. Polls taken two weeks prior to the election projected that 98.9% of the popular vote would go to Gates. Poor Zachary, who pretty much liked his hootch several times a day, didn't stand a chance. So Gates was all set to win. Supposedly it's been rumored that in a rather bizarre incident the man was accidentally ground to a pulp in a wheat-threshing machine at a campaign stop on the eve of the election. Imagine that — made into chop meat the day before you're supposed to be elected president. Hmmm… wonder if my Grandpa Taylor had something to do with that…. Anyways, Taylor won, unopposed, of course. Guess they couldn't find another body to put up against 'em.

Notoriously prone to drunken laziness Taylor held office for half a day when he gorged himself on fourteen pounds of French pastries and jugs of Indian corn whiskey and then fell asleep face-down in the White House Rose Garden for eighty-six hours. Upon awakening, he attempted his first official presidential act: the introduction of a bill requiring all visitors to the White House to do the Mexican Hat Dance with his 700 pound sister Rebecca while he, munching on his trademark sack of chocolate donuts, watched. Good Lord! I can only shake my head. Congress responded with zero "yea" votes and a rather stormy relationship between the two parties began.

A favorite prank of the senators would be to not show up to the presidential addresses but rather place muskrats, decked out in powdered wigs, in their own seats instead. Since being ridiculed from the first few days of his presidency, Taylor really snow balled out of control and had monumental jealous fits about his eleven predecessors, all of whom he was unfavorably compared to. He especially seemed to have a special hatred of George Washington (whom he referred to as "that bark-toothed Whig Sissy") and he spent much of his time trying to "one-up" the first president's celebrated accomplishments. Few Americans were amused, however, when he ordered every cherry tree east of the Mississippi to be burned to a stump, and then hurled all seventy place settings of the Presidential silverware (paid for with a staggering $56K of taxpayer money) across the Potomac River. When asked by his disbelieving father whether he was the one responsible for these acts, Taylor responded, "What do you care, *&%$# head? You'll be dead soon anyway."

His papa was probably concerned about him hocking everything too because had he not disposed of the silver this way, he surely would have lost it gambling. Within a few days of taking office, he surrendered ten priceless paintings, a bedspread given to John Quincy Adams by the King of Spain, and most of the linen to pay off poker debts. I believe it was sometime after that he spent a great deal of money on liquor, got completely soused, and fell out of the window in the oval office and was found passed out in the bushes the next morning. For some reason it really doesn't surprise me I am a descendent of this person. I can only shrug.

So that's my legacy. A cantankerous drunken man winning office by default, knocking up his Native American slave woman, angered most of the country and swindled anything of value out of the white house to fuel his gambling habit. Had he not died so quickly in office there probably would have been just the toilet and a few scraps of paper left. The biggest kicker of all is that there was a mix-up at the cemetery and his grave was given the wrong tombstone — one belonging to a Belgian flintlock. His family name: Mouskrat, French for "muskrat". Ha!

~ LIFE IN THE EMERGENCY ROOM ~

The local hospitals know my father on a first name basis. "Hi, Ron, what did you do this time?" is a popular phrase heard in every emergency room in the Hudson Valley. He's there so often they need to name a wing after him from all the business he's provided them over the years. "What's the problem" you may ask. Well, he's either accident prone or just really bad at starting a career in the suicide business.

Starting from my childhood I can count the years on which accidents my Dad has had. When the teacher asked me to recite the alphabet I'd say, "E-R." It started when he was showing me how *not* to open a car's radiator after it was running for awhile.

"See this, Carol? Don't ever open the radiator cap when it's hot — watch what happens." You guessed it — facial burns that rivaled the Joker's. That wasn't my first experience in the ER. There was the time he was showing me how to ski down the slopes of Vermont.

"Now it's very important to watch where you're going, Carol, so you don't hit a treeeeee!!" He looked like a cartoon character with his face smashed into that tree, arms and legs wrapped around it with various pieces of ski equipment strewn about the mountain. I just shook my head and wondered how he survived hitting a tree and Sonny Bono didn't — they're both the same size, I thought.

Chainsaws! There's a hot button. I can't tell you how many body parts he's cut up with a chainsaw over the years. One would think that Dr. Frankenstein must be his doctor, what with all the sewn up appendages he has. When I got my driver's permit he made sure I got full use out of it driving him to the hospital.

"Hi Carol, can you drive on over to the job site — I need your help."

"Sure, Dad, let me finish eating my sandwich and I'll be there in a half hour."

"You better come now because I'm lying under a tree."

"What?!"

"Yeah, the chainsaw got away on me and I sliced my arm just about off but I can't tell because the tree fell on me so I'm a bit stuck underneath it right now. It's a good thing the cell phone was in my other pocket," he laughs while bleeding to death. Sixteen years old and I swore like a trucker at him all the way to the hospital as he faintly kept telling me to slow down or I'd get a ticket. Can you believe that crap? As an adult whenever I hear the sound of a chainsaw I immediately begin to twitch uncontrollably. (sigh) Therapy can only do so much.

Don't even get me started on car accidents. Insurance companies now offer, "Defensive Driving around Ron" Classes. This man has totaled more cars than the Derby Raceway. The kicker is that he can roll the best trucks several times over and *still* walk away from them. He's driven one off a cliff, down a slope, landed vertically on a set of railroad tracks, and made it out of the cab before the train plowed through it. Stunt men just look at him and take notes, mumbling something about how he's putting them out of business. Absolutely amazing!

Now that he's in his sixties, retired, and recuperating from two heart attacks back-to-back, I figured his days of being Evil Knievel were over. Nope. Eating my breakfast and staring out the window at the rain last week I suddenly see his body fall from the sky. Can you believe he fell off the roof? He was working on the addition in the rain (roofs and rain don't mix well) and fell off it and into the pile of cinder blocks. I told my mother to just pour the concrete foundation on top of him and be done with it. They say cats have nine lives but watching this episode I swear I saw a mother cat telling her young, "See that guy — he's got 15 lives and counting."

~ ADRENALINE JUNKIES ARE HAZARDOUS TO YOUR HEALTH ~

Got adrenaline junky, health nuts in the family? You know the type: people that eat everything organic, probably vegetarian, don't have an ounce of fat on their bodies and typically like to do extreme sports that could kill you. My brother is one such person. He's built like a furry stick, eats birthday cake made of tofu, and partakes in dangerous activities such as rock climbing and running 100 mile races. Apparently marathons aren't challenging enough for him since they're only 29 miles long, but the toenails he lost in training would beg to differ. God made toenails for a reason; don't know what that reason could be but I assure you he doesn't want us to exercise so much that they FALL OFF!

Speaking of "falling off" let's get to the meat of this conversation. My bonehead brother fell off a mountain this past weekend! I think it was the one time in life my parents actually didn't say, "Why can't you be more like your brother?" It was on the Shawangunk Mountain in upstate NY, which is like a mole hill to him after climbing major places like Mt. Rainier. He actually fell 60 feet and lived! Can you believe that?! I think it's because he's got more hair than a bear and it acted like bubble wrap. When he goes jogging without a shirt on, people call 911 to report either Sasquatch or an escaped gorilla running down the road. So when I heard he hit the ground and **bounced**, I naturally recalled the advice from Rudolph the Red-nosed Reindeer: "Bumbles Bounce." Oh and was he ever a humble Bumble after this fiasco.

I was so happy that I was able to get out of the baby shower I had to go to with the excuse of having to go see him in the hospital at least! At any rate, he broke his femur and had to have it pinned with surgery. Since I'm stupid I had to ask which part the femur was because I was thinking of "pinned" as in "sewing" and "quilting" and naturally assumed it was his ass that broke off. I figured since cats land on their feet, most people land on their butts — makes sense. Nope. It was his leg. No internal injuries or brain damage or nothin'! Must have been all those bean sprouts and flax seed vege-burgers creating a super human Sasquatch of Steel.

I tried to find him a decent card to express how I felt but I guess Hallmark doesn't get too many requests for "Congratulations on being alive after falling off a mountain" cards. You'd think they'd be a big seller around this mountainous region. Oh, wait — they do have cards about falling off mountains — they're called "Sympathy Cards"! In this case he lived so they probably should be called unsympathetic cards. I guess I fit that unsympathetic bill considering I was smirking and muttering, "Well, it was bound to happen at some point," while everyone else was choking back tears.

I often put my foot in my mouth on such occasions especially this one when I walked into the waiting area filled with his climbing friends and yelled, "Which one of you idiots dropped my brother?" not realizing one of them actually did. My mother just kept giving me that wide eyed, "shut up" look and mouthing something to that effect. Of course it went right over my head and I just kept saying, "What? What'd I say?" The poor guy probably wanted to crawl under the table I'm sure. "It was a miscommunication," Mom said. Miscommunication??!!! Letting go of a rope somebody is dangling from - 200 ft. up solid rock - goes a little bit beyond my definition of a "miscommunication". A miscommunication is when you get a diet coke instead of a coke with your super-sized meal at the drive-thru!

Yeah that was one of my worst gafaw's. How was I to know the guy dropped him?! I thought he just slipped. It's nobody's fault really because anyone that climbs knows danger comes with the territory — hence the adrenaline rush they so crave. For the last decade I've been telling him, "Well, it's nice to know HOW you're gonna die; it's just a matter of WHEN really".

I know, I know. "How can you be so harsh, Carol?" I think my brother is actually vying for my Father's wing at the hospital…. Like father, like son. It's dangerous for me just being related to people that love that adrenaline rush because I'll be the one dropping from a heart attack from the stress of it all. Since my adrenaline junkie and accident prone relatives like to do all these extreme mountanious sports of hang gliding, rock climbing, skiing, hiking and running (causing me a ton of stress) I'm going to vote we all move to Aspen, Colorado. Then everyone's happy! They can try to kill themselves on the mountain and I'll be at the bottom completely calm and stress-free in one of the state's legal marijuana cafe's having the most delcious brownie I've ever had. Aspendam here we come!

~ UNCLE GEORGE TRIED TO MILK A BULL ONCE ~

Did I ever tell you about my Uncle George? He was the family nut-ball that as children we thought was the cat's meow and all the adults would just state that he was a little "eccentric." His first name was George although no-one used it or even knew it. He was called "Uncle" as a child by his siblings and mother, and it stuck. Uncle was a piece of work. He typically would remind you of Barney Fife from "The Andy Griffith Show". He never worked a day in his life. If people asked him what business he was in he'd say, "The Sponge business," meaning that he sponges off his niece in New York for the summer and sponges off the other niece in Florida for the winter. He made a lifetime career out of not having a job.

He was in the army for a short time. If you asked him what "company" he was in he'd say "B" Company: "B" here when it starts and "B" here when it's over! He'd show you a scar on his finger where a bullet grazed him in some war you've never heard of. Truth is … he got so damn nervous about having to go overseas that he developed an ulcer and was honorably discharged for it, thereby receiving a small stipend of spending cash monthly for the rest of his life. Since he spent the summers with my family he was the playmate for four rowdy children. He was a regular Milton Berle dressing up in ladies wigs and feather boas, asking if we wanted to play "house." When we eagerly said "yes" he'd reply, "Fine! You be the door — I'll slam ya'!"

Uncle always had these bright ideas about things that always seemed to go horribly wrong for me and my siblings. There was the time that he was in the mood for an apple pie and told me and my brother to climb an old apple tree we had in the woods behind our house. We were to shake the branches and let the really juicy ones fall down to him. I kept asking him what all the green leaves were covering the tree that we were lying on (in just our bathing suits) but he would just say, "How the hell would I know?" Well we were covered in the worst case of poison ivy ever after that. We also became bloody messes after one of his "galavantin" trips through the pricker bushes in the woods in search of blackberry bushes. If a small animal came across our path or a section of woods looked a little scary he always made one of us (at the tender age of eight mind you) go in front of him. "You go first!" "No you go first Uncle you're bigger!" "Didn't anybody ever tell you to respect your elders?" "I'm a kid for cryin' out loud — you're supposed to protect me!" Suddenly he would just turn tail and run like hell, forgetting to yell "BEES!!!!!" and leave us behind to get stung! Can you believe it?

My parents would go out for the night and say, "Now behave yourselves" and they half-heartedly were directing that at *him*. "Hey, let's make homemade ice cream!" he'd yell. We got the old hand-cranked wooden contraption out of the basement and he concocted what was supposed to be a recipe for "chocolate" ice-cream. It took us forever but the thought of the delicious treat kept us going. When it was all done he took the first spoonful right out of the container and slowly tasted his masterpiece without saying a word. He then took another spoonful, and without warning, flung it into the face of my cousin. Thus started a war of ice cream throwing that trashed the basement and ruined my father's pool table. There was ice cream on the ceiling, sofas, walls, just a horrid mess with soppy kids all worked up and soaked. After seeing what had happened he simply said, "You kids are on your own," and hijacked my little girl's bicycle to go off boozin' at the neighbors. Picture Barney Fife trying to ride a little girl's pink bicycle down a dirt road with a carton of cigs in the white flowered basket and ringing the bell the whole way. We found him in the ditch all askew and hung-over the next morning. He got so drunk he fell off the bike. He insisted over coffee it was because of the UFO in the trees that distracted him. "The birds, I'm tellin' ya, the birds in the trees all started goin' plum crazy and then all these blinking lights started to appear! I could have been killed or worse — experimented on!"

He actually tried to get me to milk a bull once when he confused it with a cow after dipping into some whiskey. That bull definitely did not like his balls grabbed when Uncle tried to milk 'em. He nearly got shish-kabobed. You see, Uncle's favorite past-time was going down the road to the old farmer's barn, eat snake meat and yell, "Carol Ann! Go in the barn and milk the cows," which meant dealing with the bull and when you're only four feet high the nightmares go on forever. Do you know how many times I got chased down by a cow, dodging cow crap, and had to dive through a barbed wire fence? All because he wanted fresh milk right from the cow.

Yea, Uncle was a character all right. There's one in every family I suppose. Now that times are changing and I'm getting older my little nieces are starting to look at me as the family nut-ball. Well, somebody's gotta carry on the tradition I suppose — might as well be crazy Auntie Carol.

~ "DON'T EVER CALL ME 'SHORTY' LEST YOU WANT YOUR KNEE CAPS BIT CLEAN OFF." ~

"Would a rose by any other name, still be a rose?" Shakespeare wrote many moons ago and even Johnny Cash's, "A boy named Sue" raises the age old question of what's in a name. Names are linked to our identities, tying us to the essence of who we are on this planet, so it's a big "ta-do" you could say. Sometimes, a person may come to be known by a nick-name based on something they've done, the way they look, or something they've said. Italian mobsters are famous for their nicknames describing what a person does, like perhaps "Cement-Shoc-Vinnie", or where their turf is, such as "Ricky-Five-Towns" and even the food they like to eat with the ever popular, "Jimmy-Bowl-of-Meatballs".

Many times people get nicknames based on their appearance such as Fat Albert, Lurch, Blondie, 3-Finger Willy, and Slim. Millions of short people five feet and under, such as myself, have forever been burdened with horrible nick-names like Shorty, Short-stuff, Midget, Miss Inch, or Shortcake. "Half Pint" was made a favorite nickname for little Laura Ingalls by her Pa in "Little House on the Prairie". I do remember a group of girlfriends I hung around with in high school who tried calling me Shorty once and I immediately vetoed that. "What the heck are we supposed to call you........Moose?" they said. Now that was a name I could get behind — completely opposite and kinda' quirky. So Moose it was for the duration of my teen years, always stumping people when they would yell, "Hey Moose!" and a pathetic little tic-tac of a girl would squeak out an "I'm over here."

My entire family strangely enough would name a child onc name on their birth certificates and then call them a different name the rest of their lives with no rhyme or reason. For instance, it wasn't until I was in high school that I learned that all these years my mother went by the name of "Judy" but on her birth certificate it was really "Eileen". I happened to see her driver's license one day: "Who the heck is 'Eileen', Ma? You runnin' from the law or somethin'?" Apparently they named her after some rich Aunt that demanded she be named for her and so they put it on the birth certificate but called her "Judy" for spite and also that she looked like a "Judy Friendly", a term for a happy child back then.

So then she unravels this odd tale of how my Aunty Sandy's real name is "Alexandria", my Aunt Midge's real name was "Emma", that the woman I've called Aunt Peg for the duration of my life was actually named "Julia". I was rather shocked by this news. "Ma, are you *sure* you don't have skeletons in the closet you want to tell me about? Hmmmm?"

For years my cousin Richard would call me "Jimmy Mike" because one day my father was cutting my brother's hair and I wanted mine cut and Dad went a little scissor happy, which made my mother very unhappy since I kept being mistaken for a boy. Richard rubbed salt on the wound by poking fun and laughing up a storm, and calling me Jimmy Mike. So, my mother put me in pink dresses for a year till my hair grew long enough for barrettes. I could have stuck a fork in my eye. No wonder I've always felt an aversion to pink dresses as an adult. "I musta' been kidnapped by gypsies," I reasoned with myself.

Then there are the gross nicknames you get in college that have to do with either sex, a fraternity/sorority, drugs, or a disgusting bodily function. For years people would ask me why my parents named me "Suki" when I wasn't Asian. After explaining that my real name was Carol, and being told I look nothing like a Carol, (which begs the question of what the hell is a "Carol" suppose to look like) I had to tell the sick tale. Upon turning 21 years old I finally had my first legal beer as a rite of passage, thereby also experiencing vomiting from said rite of passage. As my unsympathetic friends winced and asked what I had for dinner I blurted out, "Sukiyaki". Well, "Suki" stuck like cling wrap and I went by it for almost a decade. No wonder my self image is so messed up — my whole adult life has been based on puke.

So there you have it — a name defines you as a person and shapes your life and who you are and will become. So all you couples out there expecting babies please don't name your children stupid names they will hate you for later.

~ THE INCURABLE
SHOPPING DISEASE ~

I have to tell you about my cousin Becky. She has a rather unique gift about her that most would find remarkable and others perhaps bordering on criminal. She has a "Shopping Disease". She has developed into an art form the ability to somehow go into a mall and get whatever she wants for "free". The ability to actually talk store managers into giving her merchandise for nothing. It's true. You have to see her in action.

You ever go into a store, see an item you bought years earlier, and tell the store manager yours broke and he should give you a replacement piece for free without the item or the receipt? Becky has. You ever see a sign for 20% off an item and argue with the store manager about his sign and walk out with a 70% reduced item? Yup, Becky has. Store managers must cringe when they see her coming. There should be a support group for people like this.

The first time she exemplified these incredible super human powers of persuasion was in college. I was coming for a visit and she wanted to fix up her apartment a little so she went out to a department store and bought some things. One item was a yellow area rug that you can cut up to fit the size of your bathroom. So, she measured out where the toilet was and where the tub and sink were too, onto the carpet. She decided it'd be easier to cut the carpet upside down so she turned it over and cut out the carpet where it would fit around the facilities. Well, you can imagine what happened. She turned the rug back over right-side up and couldn't figure out why the tub, sink, and toilet were all backwards in respect to where she cut them out on the carpet. Well the thought of blowing a good $30.00 bucks was too much to bear so she ripped out the scotch tape and taped it back together as best as she could even though it was a complete cut-up horror show, folded it back up, and brought the whole abomination back to the store. She told them "It has a slight rip in it. It came that way," and they took it back and gave her a new one. Can you believe that?!

As the years went by she honed her talents and moved up to the big leagues of her little independent enterprise. The women in my family decided to spend the weekend in Pennsylvania at the outlet stores. Outlet stores are like a pilgrimage to the consumer's holy land. Becky decided to buy a pair of jeans for her boyfriend. She got a cheap pair of jeans at a cost of $7.00 at some unknown store. Not only were they the wrong size but they were obviously of inferior quality. So she brings them to a reputable store in the Mall, no receipt, and demands an even exchange for a $35.00 pair of Levis…and get's it! That's impossible for most people like you and me. When we go they never give us anything without a receipt and they fight with us tooth and nail over a lousy $5.00.

I think my favorite scheme yet was how she went out to a very big chain store to buy a bedspread. So she goes to the store, buys a bedspread, sheets, shams, skirt, the whole works for $200.00. A year goes by and she notices that they have faded in color and have become ragged and shabby. So she goes out buys the exact same ensemble all over again. She goes home, takes the new spread and sheets etc., puts them on the bed and takes the old set of stuff, wraps them up and puts them back in the zippered plastic bag. She brings them back to the same store and said she didn't like them and wanted her money back. So they credit her card and Voila — new sheets. Are you getting disgusted yet? Are you taking notes? Or perhaps someone is sending the police over to my cousin's house right now?

Sooooo… as the years went by she became the master. Now this is an advanced skill so please don't try this at home. Her #1 rule is to wait them out. She waits until they get so exhausted trying to respond to her crazy logic that they give in, give her what she wants, and push her out the door to shut her up. At last I checked, her latest venture was going into a department store perfume counter and asking for a sample of some $150 perfume. She argues that her toddler is with her and doesn't want the chemicals to affect his brain. So she pulls an empty glass bottle out of her purse and they actually give her a good 4oz. of the stuff — a good $50 worth at least – so she can try it on later when her child is napping in another room. [rolling my eyes and shaking my head] So now she's got a month's worth of expensive perfume for nothin'.

I'm sure any time now I'll see her face either in the police blotter or on some Shopping Disease Website asking for support and donations to find a cure.

~ WHAT BIG EYES YOU
HAVE, GRANDMA ~

Grandmothers, Grandmothers…. What to say about Grandmothers. I've been thinking about my own grandmother who we call, "Nan" or "Nanny". I personally like to call her by her first name, which gets me an angry glare from my mother.

She's far from the sweet little old lady type though. I'd say she's like that cartoon old lady, "Maxine" on all the greeting cards and calendars. The type of crotchety that makes you love her one minute and the other minute you want to push her down the stairs. She complains all day long, says inappropriate things that get under your skin, puts her foot in her mouth often, and occasionally gets herself into odd predicaments. One morning having coffee on the front porch I thought I was seeing things when I saw her attempting to run with her walker from a bucking cow hell bent on running her down. Either I was still hung over or that coffee was bad, I reasoned, as I tossed the cup of Jo into the bushes. Apparently the cows got loose from the farm next door but how these lazy docile creatures came to being provoked enough to chase my Nan across the front yard I have no idea. I guess her irritating way affects not only humans but animals too.

I lived with her as a child for a short period when I was four years old and my parents were in the process of building a house. She was my first babysitter. My parents would get up and go to work and her and I would each have our own cup of coffee and read the paper side by side, her with a cigarette hanging out of her mouth. There I was learning to read except it wasn't about little boy blue but rather all the crime and corruption the *New York Post* could offer while also stunting my growth with Maxwell House. Her chain smoking probably had nothing to do with my asthma I'm sure. She and I spent many years existing solely on Entenmanns — she bought so much you'd think she owned stock in it!

I also lived with her for a couple years in my twenties. I'd take her shopping and then we'd go to the early bird special dinner up on "the avenue" which was the main drag. Her and her friends would flip if they didn't get dinner by 4pm. They'd have strawberry daiquiris, open face turkey sandwiches with stuffing and cranberry sauce, and laugh about the old days. One night she said she wanted to try something different and ordered the "Chicken **Condom** Bleu". When the waitress looked a little startled at her verbal slip I couldn't help but blurt out, "I think that might be a bit too rubbery for you, Nan" with a laugh. All those old ladies just stared at me deadpan like I was a stupid kid and sneered to stop being a smart ass. A lecture about every little thing I'm doing wrong came after that as they'd go on and on about me staying out too late and giving the cow's milk away for free and how at my age they all had ten kids and made stone soup for a dozen people that lasted for three days cuz it was the depression and they were damn glad to have that stone soup and who do I think I am anyways. Apparently after seventy-five you don't have much of a sense of humor. Those days, like two typical roommates, we'd fight like cats and dogs and she'd insist she called me a "witch" and not a "bitch" when I just KNOW that wasn't the case.

So now twenty years later since she lives with my Mom and Dad I stop over to spend time with her. She's gotten even more ornery now over the years (which I didn't think was possible) and still drives us up the wall. She'll read every business and road sign as we drive down the road and repeat the same stories a zillion times in a day and thinks it's Easter when it's Christmas.

Strangely enough I find myself succumbing to her madness from time to time as I start repeating some of the odd little sayings she has. When I look into a mirror now I find myself saying "I look like 'who did it and ran'!" Whenever she finishes something, like bringing her dish to the sink, she says, "Good, good good." After hearing it a thousand times I found myself saying "good, good, good" the other day at work when I finished a stack of paperwork which make me go nuts and want to stick a fork in my eye. If she's had a busy day going to the senior center to "gibby-gab" (another phrase) with her friends she'll say she was "goin' like a house on fire all day" which I've said to people and they looked at me quite oddly. And wouldn't you know it but whenever I can't win a verbal disagreement with someone I throw my hands up, look to heaven and say, "You win, I lose!" which pretty much ends the conflict because both of us would burst out laughing thinkin' of how Nan states this signature calling card phrase about twenty times a day in cranky frustration. She'd then storm off wheeling herself down the hall and slamming her door shut to obviously punish us with the silent treatment. This usually makes my mother say, "Give me the strength, Lord"

Now that she's ninety-four she can't see or hear very well, gets confused often, and you never know if she's gonna laugh or cry. When she sees all her little great grandchildren running around and asks me for the fifth time if the little boy is mine, or whose little girl is that, we just tell her "Don't worry Nan, there's not going to be a test on this later." She gets flustered so I tell her she's with her family and they all love her and that's the important thing. Strangely enough most days I'm the only name she can remember and she tells me often that I'm her favorite when I'm lifting her out of bed and changing her. Then she gets cranky and yells that I'm being too rough and would never make it as a nurse. Sigh…. I guess we're a pair, the two of us.

~ AN AUTOMOBILE LOVE AFFAIR ~

Don't ya' just love a good car show? There's been a few around lately and I try to go whenever I can. My love affair with cars was inspired by my father. As a typical greaser of the 50's he used to race hot rods. He'd come up to Orange County from Jersey and race his 55 Buick Century and loves to revisit his glory days from time to time. When I was a kid he built a dune buggy complete with a roll bar and its fiberglass was a sparkling baby blue. He would load up my mother and all us kids and cruise the streets of Jersey, and from then on I was hooked on the automobile as one sweet ride.

When I was a freshman in high school my older brother was a senior and he had a classic convertible MG. I'd beg him to give me a ride to school in it and sometimes he would unless I wore my red suede candies and neon orange plastic balloon pants. "Oh, you're riding the bus today, Carolann, 'cause there's no way you're getting into my car looking like that....and DON'T say hello to me in the hallways either," he'd say shaking his head.

When I finally was able to drive a car myself my father was a wreck and decided to start to teach me a little bit about cars especially after I destroyed the first car he gave me — a little red Pinto. He had to pick me up on a deserted road one night because my car wouldn't move. I not only had forgotten to put gas in it but apparently I didn't realize you needed to check things called "the oil" and when smoke comes out it's called, "overheating" because there wasn't any water in it. For years after that he drilled into my head, "Gas, Water, Oil" and wrote a home-made sign saying "Gas, Water, Oil" in big red letters which hung from the rearview mirror to remind me that I'm an idiot. "What are you going to do every single time you go into a gas station, Carol Ann?" "Check the gas, water and oil, Dad."

From then on he worried about me getting stuck and made me practice changing the tire over and over again in the event of a flat. He would even time me on a stopwatch. Why I couldn't just carry around a can of "fix a flat" like every other teenager I don't know. His idea of teaching me car repairs was, "Listen to the engine.... the part that's making the funny noise you remove, walk into Napa and say, 'I don't know what this is but give me one just like it for a Chevy Impala', and then you put the new one in the same way you took the old one out and that's basically the gist of things."

After that I started to enjoy working on cars with my father and became the son he never had. (Don't tell my brothers I said that.) We had some great discussions over bleeding the brakes, figuring out the gap size for my spark plugs, changing the distributor cap and accidentally starting the car on fire... ahh... good times. I was the only girl in tenth grade that knew what size engine she had. When I went to the parts store for a new oil filter, the chauvinistic pig behind the counter says, "I don't suppose you would know what size engine you have there, sugar pie?" Without blinking I say, "3.4 liter engine." He laughs and ribs his buddy and says, "Wow, I'm shocked you knew that." I cocked my head, raised one brow and replied, "Yeah, well then it's sure to blow your little pea brain when I jack the car up and put this filter in myself, I imagine." It was then I realized the value of what my father taught me as years to come when I knew exactly when a mechanic was feeding me a line of crap, and I knew exactly what was wrong with my car, what needed to be done and how much it should really cost. With just a sniff I instantly know when my car is a quart low and that the odd sound I've been hearing means the belt needs changing.

So it's no wonder I marvel at the antique cars at all the shows. I enjoy the stages of the automobile from the chitty-chitty-bang-bang cars to the stylish 50's muscle cars and marvel at the sleek curves of the sporty Camaro. It's amazing how clean the engines are at these shows — they're cleaner than my best china. Every car has a story to tell and the owners love to tell a yarn or two about them. People who really love restoring them to such works of art should be proud of themselves for keeping alive a piece of history for the rest of us to enjoy. I recently was told I have some readers up North that are restoring a military jeep and I salute you. My father is currently restoring a World War II Willy and having a time of it. Takes a lot of time and patience to recreate the past.

Just like my father did before me, when seeing an antique car passing us on the road I yell, "Look, look, kids, there's a 57 Chevy! What a beauty! Did you see that?" I look forward to the day I can pass on some car skills to my kids but, hell, by that time we might all be in hovercraft spaceships and they'll be saying to me, "What was it like growing up with cars, Mom?"

~ CHAPTER FIVE ~

RANDOM THOUGHTS OF
A MID-LIFE MELTDOWN

There comes a moment in time when you hit the wall and realize you might be having a mid-life crisis, a nervous breakdown or both. As we grow older gaining wisdom and experience while trying to keep our brood alive, it's amazing we don't all go cuckoo bananas..

.... oh wait…we do…it's called going senile…

~ WELCOME TO THE MENTAL BREAKDOWN PORTION OF YOUR LIFE ~

I've had **way** too much caffeine and stress today. I now completely understand, without a shadow of a doubt, why my mother used to tell my siblings and I that she was just gonna get in the car and drive away and never come back. I believe the formal wording for it is "nervous breakdown."

Oh, I already know it's inevitable that I'll eventually have one. It's now a question of "when." There are some days the drumming of my heart is so loud I have to lie down on the floor for fear my head will explode and my veins will just burst from my appendages and make a mess of the place. It's at those moments I just stare at the ceiling and ask myself, "Is this it? Is this the breakdown? Is this how it feels?" If you've been there you **know** what I'm talking about. It's almost as if you can actually hear the nerves frying up like a pound of bacon, your eyes just pop out like poached eggs, and all you hear is some old farm lady ringing a loud clanging triangle yellin' "Breakfast!" I imagine for the viewer of such moments it must be a frightening experience. When my mother had such moments my siblings and I would just get really quiet and try to figure out who amongst us was gonna tell Dad when he got home that Mom finally went cuckoo bananas, packed it in and left.

At moments when I have these little energy power failures I start to do a 'root cause analysis' as to why this all happened. It gives me something to do while staring at the ceiling waiting for the panic attack to pass. My analysis has led me to believe that children and men are your basic culprits in the cake batter of life thrown in there like freaky rainbow sprinkles that drive us to the edge. They're like a fine soufflé but unfortunately the majority of them backfire, blow up the oven, and come out a floopy mess. Yep. That's what men are — flopped soufflés that whine almost as bad as your children.

I think I realized it for the first time in the seventh grade when I saw this kid Noel try sucking his turnips through his soda straw in the cafeteria. This made a huge impression on me; not because he used a straw but because it was "turnips." I mean, my God, who the hell likes turnips soooo much to even eat them with a *fork,* let alone risk an aneurysm trying to suck them up with a straw? Now chocolate pudding I could see; turnips — no way. What the hell was he thinking? How could he possibly think that it would work or that it would somehow cause him the slightest bit of pleasure in doing so? He even looked like a turnip - short with red hair and very stubborn. Maybe he was the mothership of all turnips but in human form. "There's something wrong with the male portion of this program" is what my middle school mind assessed of the situation.

So we've already established that men and children are major root causes to such mental breakdowns; let's stir the pot further, throwing in clothes and weight. Hell, why not? Both are my arch enemies bent on destroying me for sure. No matter what I put on to wear it won't fit and looks like crap. "I didn't know the dollar store now sold women's clothing" is a remark I've heard before. You ever wake up and can't find a thing to wear for work and you go through all the dirty laundry looking for the *one* shirt that will make your world stable again, and you can't find it so then you have to pick something else. The only problem is that "everything else" is wrinkled beyond your wildest imagination and you convince yourself that "it'll take too long" to iron. So then you spend the next hour trying on every piece of crap gathering dust for the last two years and three sizes ago, in some whacked-out frenzy that leaves you feeling like some old, out of date, tub of goo. I finally got disgusted one day and went in my pajamas dragging three outfits behind me and announced to my boss that I was waiting to be inspired. I got written up for that one; which is the equivalent to being sent to the principal's office for throwing spit balls.

It was during one of these little mental breakdowns that I got a huge scar on my abdomen that took about twenty-five stitches. All I'm gonna say is that it involves a pickle fork and a pizza cutter. As a result I will never eat Twinkies again. I could hyperventilate just *thinking* about that catastrophe. Oy. I think I need to lie down now.

~ "IT'S ALWAYS SOMETHING!" ~

You ever notice that just when you get on a roll and things might actually start looking up for once, something always happens to put you back two spaces again?! As one of my favorite comediennes, Gilda Radner from Saturday Night Live, would always say, "It's always something!" Life has a way of throwing a monkey wrench into the best laid plans.

My last doozy of a week is a prime example of "It's always something". I thought I was getting ahead and keeping an organized schedule of running various errands like picking up the kids' portrait pictures etc... After driving the half hour to the big bad box store I picked up the envelope of pictures and was glad that I could finally cross that off my list. Unfortunately it got put back on the list when my daughter accidentally spilled my coffee all over the portraits ruining every last one of them.

Then I had finally gotten around to changing the burnt out light bulb in one of the bathroom fixtures I had put off for months. I got the ladder out of the garage, and risked my life trying to balance on the top rung - on tippy toe - all whilst not getting electrocuted. After putting the ladder back in the garage, I sighed at another task completed and went to flip the switch to the stairwell light and ~zap~ it blows. Grrr…. How the hell do you change a ceiling light bulb in a stairwell?! Who's idea was it to put a light that high up in a stairwell anyways?! Unless I'm dating the Jolly Green Giant, that's one light bulb that ain't gettin' changed. The kids will just have learn to walk down the stairs in the dark.

Also this week I happened to notice I had an extra hundred bucks in my account and all the bills were paid. Wow — extra money at the end of the month — who woulda thunk it?! Hmm… whatever shall I spend it on? Maybe I'll take the kids to a movie, and have dinner at someplace other than McDonalds. Well that thought came to an abrupt end when I got into my car and realized the motorized driver seat was jammed with one of the kids' thermos under the seat and wouldn't move forward. It was all the way in the back position and since I'm from Munchkinland I had to practically lay down to reach the gas pedal and still strain to see over the wheel at the same time. Not only was I worried about driving off the side of the Shawangunk Mountains but I scared the hell out of all the other drivers thinking the car was driving itself and went by the name of "Christine". So replacing the seat motor due to "death by thermos" took that extra cash toot sweet.

Pretty much after that the rest of the week went kaplooey and went beyond going two spaces back and was rapidly moving to "game over". The digital camera somehow accidentally deleted all the Christmas pictures. Then somebody told me to rub an onion on my car windshield to avoid frost ….not only did it not work but now I can't get the onion smell out of the car and the onion juice smeared all over the windshield won't come off. After dealing with that I got into a fight with a pencil sharpener. My daughter had a broken pencil and some sort of a bead got stuck in the pencil sharpener and I cut my finger on a knife trying to get it out. When that didn't work I tried to whittle the pencil to a point so she could finish her homework and cut another finger doing that. I finally ran out of band-aids and fingers, gave up, and gave her a pen to use. Then I got a nasty teacher note home scolding me for letting her use a pen.

I almost didn't mind so much by the time the hook on the bathroom door fell off leaving a gaping hole in the door. It's not bad enough that you get no peace in the bathroom with kids always bursting in on you, but now they don't even need to do that. They just look through the hole and whine… "Whatcha' dooooin' Mommy???"

Yup, it's always somethin' alright. I can almost hear Gilda laughing in heaven right now.

~ "WHAT THE HELL?" ~

You ever have one of those "What the Hell" kinda' moments? Like out of nowhere while waiting for the bus, you get smacked in the face with a boat oar by a medieval gnome hiding in the bushes. "What the Hell?! Didn't see that comin," you might say. I've had a lot of moments like that.

I think it all started in elementary school when I came home off the school bus with nothing on but my Duckie Underoos and a trench coat. No — I wasn't a little flasher in the making; I simply lost my dress. "How the hell did you lose the clothes off your back, young lady?" my mother wanted to know. It was a long story involving a tutu, smacking my head on the floor, and my dress winding up as a flag that my brother waved up and down the aisle of the school bus. My first, "What the hell?" moment.

Prom! There's a hot button filled with "What the Hell" moments. There's always some idiot wearing a three-musketeers outfit or a chick that made her dress out of duct tape with a matching purse. One kid will be having a full out, streaming tears, tomato-faced meltdown out the side door in their purple tux screaming into the cell phone, "You don't give a @#$% about me!!" Ahhh…good times. It reminds me of my own, "What the Hell 'Prom' moment." Wearing a white gown I wanted to make sure I had at least some color so I wasn't so pasty white. So the day of the prom I skipped school and decided to lie on the back porch to get a great tan. It was kind of overcast so I got out some tin-foil and wrapped it all over the lounge chair. Then I covered myself in vegetable oil and put myself out to bake for 90 minutes. Well, dip me in butter, I got color alright — a nice lobster red in a white dress. Then when my date showed up just as red, we were a perfect match — a couple of candy canes. Then when we were seated at the wrong table with the weird kids nobody knew — it was just icing on the cake. Sigh, the pain still hasn't healed….

My most frustrating "What the Hell?!" moment happened when I went to deliver my second child and the nurse tells me they changed their policy and they don't give as much of the epidural that they did two years earlier when I delivered my daughter high as a flippin' kite on that stuff. Words cannot describe the rage as I ripped that poor woman a new one telling her what she could do with her flippin' policy. She didn't say a word but instead stuck a needle in me with something called "Stadol." Well, let me tell you! I asked for another round of that Stadol stuff and wanted to know if it came in six packs to go. So it started out a very frustrated "What the Hell" moment but turned into a giggly-high, "What the Hellll, Man…" kinda moment.

Now there are all kinds of sub-categories of the "What the Hell" moment. There's the "Delicious-Gossipy" category when you tell your girlfriend about the blow-out argument the neighbors had in the driveway and with a raised eyebrow and shaking her head, "Mmmm Mmm, Girl, what the hell…". Then there's the "Road Rage" category whereby that crazed old lady side-swipes your car and when you both pull over she tells you she's going blind and is on the way to the eye doctor. You clench your teeth and grumble "What the Hell" under your breath as you consider backing your car over her. At times you may want to graduate to the ever popular, "What the Fuck?!" which is when you walk out of the bathroom to find that your adorable children have painted everything with peanut butter. Peanut butter all over the dog, your expensive big screen TV, inside the Blu-Ray, each other, the walls, leather couch, the carpet….. everywhere. Boy, and if there's truly evil in this world it's getting peanut butter off of anything. Try cleaning a hunk of it off a knife that's been in a sink full of water for awhile. It's just nasty… [gag]… not to mention almost impossible to get off of anything. It just won't dissolve! So this definitely qualifies for a mind-blowing, "What the Fuck!" moment.

You too can have your own "What the Hell?!" moment. Just look around; they're everywhere waiting to strike at just the right moment like a crouching medieval gnome waiting in a bush with a boat oar.

~ THESE PEEVES ARE NO PETS ~

We all have them — those special little nuggets that happen in daily life that just drive us crazy. The first usage of the popular phrase "pet peeve" was in 1919. The term originated from the word 'peeve', a variation of the 14th-century word 'peevish,' meaning ornery or ill-tempered.

In researching this subject I stumbled upon a few websites devoted solely to allowing people to vent their pet peeve frustrations lest they walk into a McDonalds and blow a dozen people away with a semi-automatic because they didn't want pickles on their burger. So of course, being the compassionate person I am I thought I could lend a hand, address some of the worst ones mentioned, and help in finding a solution.

1. "People talking on Cell phones while driving their cars." Easy one! Electronic devices could be installed that zap people with a 1,000 volts of electricity if they hold the phone to their ears. Okay, what's next?

2. "All people bug me — especially ones that are breathing." I found this to be an interesting one on a website. I'm not here to judge but I would highly recommend this person enter into the career of "mortician" since dead people usually aren't breathing and won't bug her as much perhaps.

3. "When men leave the toilet seat up." I like the direct approach with this one. In my house I leave a loaded revolver next to the toilet with a sign stating specifically what will happen if that occurs. Haven't had a seat left standing at attention yet, by golly, so I guess it's workin'.

4. "My kids keep whining for candy at the grocery check-out lane." I have found that calmly telling children that sugar is not good for them simply doesn't work — it doesn't seem to make sense to them. What to do? Lie, damn it, Lie! I told my kids they weren't candy bars but actually doggie treats — not a peep out of them since. Thank God they can't read yet.

5. "I can't stand it when people in the far left lane on the highway are doing way below the speed limit and we have to pass on the right." This is a common problem that annoys everyone except the person in the fast lane which is usually an elderly person just doing their job in trying to keep the rest of us honest. I hereby propose that car makers should take a tip from the toy makers of "Hot Wheels" and install electronic prongs on the bottom of cars. When a car goes below the speed limit whilst in the left lane, it goes into autopilot and immediately switches them into the right hand lane. Hey — I only come up with the ideas.

6. "The toilet paper roll is put on the wrong way or no-one ever puts a new one on the dispenser." What is it with bathroom and car etiquette? Those are the two areas that people complained about the most! Says a lot about our society — we like to keep it moving — in both areas! Ha! Well, there's really only one solution to the toilet paper problem: Use a blow dryer.

Now, I know you are wondering what MY biggest pet peeve is, right? Of course you are! I used to hate getting behind a school bus on the way to work in the morning when I'm already running late. Last week going up the side of the mountain I not only was behind a school bus, but in front of them was a cop, a horse trailer and a truck carrying a steam roller threatening to break loose. In the back of my mind was my girlfriend telling me the night before that she had a dream I got run over by a steam roller. I laughed thinking "what are the chances of THAT happening".

As I watched the steam roller snap a line and begin to shake violently I gulped and told God I will never gripe about pet peeves again! So what's my pet peeve? Nada; nothin'; I'm good. (Don't want to tempt fate…)

~ "HEY, NO CUTTING IN LINE, LADY!" ~

I was recently watching my kids in their swim class as the instructor lined them up to jump into the pool. "Oh, man," my brother-in-law says, "I've never liked line cutters; it's always bugged me since I was a kid. Now look — my daughter's cutting everyone in line." Sure, enough, like "Veruca Salt" in "Willy Wonka and the Chocolate Factory", screaming "I want a Golden Goose, Daddy, and I want it NOW" my darling little niece pushed herself to the front of the line to jump in first. I couldn't help my chuckle though because she just hadn't yet been taught about "standing in line."

I'm pretty sure one of the first things they teach you in pre-school is the concept of getting in line. Everyone gets in a line and you wait your turn. Just about everywhere you go there's a wait and you have to deal with it in all fairness whether you're two or ninety-two. There's a line at the movie theatre, McDonalds, the post office, and of course the mother of all lines — the DMV.

We have "country line dancing" and the "conga line" which are activities we do after hitting the "beer line" and then afterwards we make a bee-line for the "bathroom line". You never want to be in a "line-up" which could be a result of selling a few "lines" and the "bottom line" to that is five years in the "penitentiary line". People make a living on an "assembly line", and when that line ends they move on over to the "unemployment line", which is a line of BS. And don't ya hate it when you're in the grocery store line staring at the nutball in front of you with fifty coupons, six screaming kids, writing a check and thinking, "Damn, I got on the wrong line."

I guess you could say lines are a big part of our society. So basically when someone breaks that rule and cuts the line it pretty much chaps your hide with good reason. How many times has it driven you nuts when you're in a line of stopped traffic on the highway and a motorcycle just drives up the yellow line cutting everyone? Don't ya just hate it when you've waited two hours on a line to get tickets and then a little old lady in a wheelchair gets wheeled up to get the last two tickets selling out the show you wanted to see for six months?

I, myself, recently had an altercation at a Dunkin' Donuts regarding line cutting. This woman behind me outright cuts me in line, giving the clerk her order when he asked "Who's next" and instead of apologizing with an, "Oh, I'm sorry, you're right, you were next", she gives me a snide remark. So I pushed passed her, gave the clerk my order and explained to my children, "This woman is what you would call, 'rude', kids, which is a fancy word for someone that is just not nice, so don't ever cut anyone in line — wait your turn." Suddenly my second grader breaks out into song, singing Taylor Swift's "All you're ever gonna be is mean." I couldn't help but smirk while ordering her an extra donut.

~ THE DIFFERENCES BETWEEN MEN AND WOMEN ~

I'm freezing. I'm always cold it seems. I have thin blood… hmpf… it's probably the only thing on me that's thin. They say women have thinner blood than men. They're walking around in their underwear in the middle of winter and we're ready for the Eskimo fashion show. At my house I'm the one sitting on the room heater with enough grill marks on my butt that I could pass for a steak. Ahh…. Just one of the many differences between men and women.

Women, for example, are quite concerned with their appearance. In this pursuit we have endured endless hours of Size 2 Aerobics Instructors drilling us like soldiers screaming, *"C'mon, Ladies!!! You*

Grew It – You Lift It!!!!!" which then leads us to a thousand bucks blown in therapy for our depression and self-esteem issues. If there is something out there that can make us smarter, more attractive, thinner, or younger we have tried it regardless of the repercussions. "Zeniflat can help you lose up to 30 pounds in a month. It works with your system to help rid your body of unwanted fat and harmful cholesterol that clogs your arteries. Zeniflat may not be for everyone. Pregnant women and women who wish to become pregnant should not take Zeniflat due to risk of horribly disfiguring birth defects resulting in babies with nine heads. Zeniflat may cause bleeding from the eyes and increased nose snot. Because Zeniflat blocks one-third of the fat from foods you eat, you may experience increased bowel movements with an oily discharge with the inability to control them (especially in the middle of important business meetings), risk of seizures, liver damage, and heart disease. People on anti-depressants should not take this drug due to the high potential to commit suicide. Zeniflat may cause shortness of breath, dizziness, migraine headaches, and big crater-like warts in the middle of your face. Zeniflat isn't for everyone but it is for some people and they love it!! So get back into a new slimmer, sexier you and start really living the good life again!!" Yea, right, like that's a product I want to just run right out and get a gallon of. Hey I might not be able to control all my bodily functions but I'll look totally hot and sexy!! Unfortunately it might end my social life entirely if I'm on a date and I accidentally crap my pants. The date is pretty much over right there.

Men, on the other hand, also have their weaknesses too. Using my brothers and father as an example I must say they have collected some of the most ridiculous pieces of crap from garage sales and auctions that have filled the basement to bursting capacity — a really messed up graveyard of broken items that "just need a little work." Some of these oddities include an oxen yolk, old trumpet, a 1920's barber's chair, a telephone booth, a juke box, a 7-up machine, two rusted cook stoves, a zillion old roller-skates, banjos that were so desperately wanted – played once – and thrown on the heap and (of course) massive boxes of comic books that are "worth a lot of money" but which they will never sell. I'm not even gonna try to explain the crane and the bull-dozer my father brought home. Some men buy trinkets, my father buys life-size Tonka trucks that he can boyishly drive around the property pushing dirt around.

Don't even get me started on the whole "car" thing. No matter what the circumstances, when greeting a male member of the family, inevitably one of the first questions will be, "How's the car running?" I am reminded of a situation last fall whereby my father was rushed to the hospital after having a seizure. My brother picked me up in the middle of the night and we made the two hour trek to see him in the hospital. It's 2 a.m. and there's dead silence in the car with me assuming both of us were consumed with worry and prayer until he says, "How's the car running?" I gave him my jaw-dropped stunned look. "What in God's name is wrong with you???!!! Our father is hanging by a thread and all you can think to say to me is 'How's the car running'? Is that all men think about?!" "No - that's not all we think about," he responds. Dead silence as I patiently wait to see what else you men think about which basically means it was quiet for two hours.

We finally arrive at the hospital and I rush into the emergency room in tears to see my poor father and when I come to his bedside he is gasping trying to tell me something and finally is able to get it out. "How's the car running, Carol?" I just looked at my brother and shook my head. Yep….. a lot of differences between men and women……

~ THE 25 YEAR REUNION ~

So I had my 25th year high school reunion this past weekend. Holy smokes, I can't believe how some people have changed and I didn't recognize them and others who eerily never aged. Pretty much everyone was shocked that I was a humor columnist because I basically was viewed as the shy girl in the corner at the back of the room. What they didn't know was that I was spewing sarcastic crap about everyone else in the room to the one or two losers sitting next to me. If there's one thing I couldn't stand back then and even now was being snubbed by perky blonde cheerleaders with big boobs. Nothing's changed — I still made wise cracks in the corner but at least this time I had alcohol in my hand and their boobs were now having an affair with their belly buttons.

I was really happy that there were about seventy people there because our class was a pretty tight group with the majority of them being rather nice people. It was wonderful to catch up with old friends but it was bittersweet to find out that fourteen people from our class had passed away. How time flies so quickly and you wake up to find yourself middle-aged. Due to the recent invention of social websites at least people can keep up with their old classmates. I've been able to re-connect with some of them on Facebook, which my Aunt says is the work of the devil and should be called "Sexbook" because it breaks up marriages. People do like to see whatever happened to their first loves, I suppose.

The things you find out when you go back down memory lane floored me though. One of my closest friends who turned out to be a nurse confessed that she had stolen my car on numerous occasions throughout my high school career. Apparently her and another friend somehow "borrowed" my car keys at lunch time and made copies. They went joy riding with my car every day skipping classes while I dutifully attended mine. To hear her talk about how stressful it was to make sure they got close to the same parking spot and would scrounge for nickels and dimes in their purses to put the gas gauge back where it was, killed me. Can you believe this?!! I don't know if I was ticked off because I apparently was the victim of grand theft auto or that they didn't invite me on their wild escapades through the countryside on a weekly basis. She said that I wasn't asked to join in because somebody needed to get good grades to help the rest of the "gang" cheat so they could graduate. I wonder if the patients she's cutting into daily would like to know their head nurse cheated her way through school in a stolen car. OY!!!!

What's really a kick in the head is that my guidance counselor told me I'd never graduate high school let alone go to college. "I think it's a waste of my time putting these college applications in for you, Miss Nelson, because you're not going to be accepted into any college. If you did I'm 100% sure you'd fail out the first semester," he said. He continued to stress my lack of skills in math and science and that's what colleges stress heavily he said. "Listen, I've wanted to be a writer since I was in kindergarten and the only thing I need to know about math and science is how to balance my checkbook and to get my butt indoors to beat the cumulus rain clouds." I might have failed math but I had all "A's" in English. I often wondered if he told all the math freaks that they needed to improve their grammar — which to me is far more useful than calculus.

After I got my Masters degree I saw him late one night. It was around midnight on a deserted dirt road and he was having difficulty changing a tire on his car. I slowed down, rolled down my window and yelled, "I got my Masters degree you @#$%*&!!!!!!" and sped off. Do I feel bad about that? Hell no! Every time I hit rock bottom in my life I told myself I was going to prove him wrong, pulled up my Wonder Woman panties, and got back on my feet. Thinking about it now 20+ years later I crack up laughing because he probably had no idea who I was or what the hell I was talking about. I definitely did not see HIM at the reunion. One thing he was right about though — I still can't balance my checkbook.

Already my fellow alumni are planning the next reunion for the next decade. That one will be more like comparing surgeries, who's had a heart attack, just retired, has grandchildren now, still sporting their own teeth, gotten Botox, or been disowned by their own children…

~ MOMMY NEEDS SLEEP ~

I'll give you one guess as to what time of day I'm writing about this topic. Every night like clockwork I wake up at 3 a.m. I think it's a disease I caught from my infant's feeding schedule that I haven't yet shaken and she's six now. Like a delusional idiot I wander about the house looking for something to do to make me sleepy.

I search from room to room for the TV remote and finally realize after twenty minutes it's been in my hand the whole time. When I actually do wind up falling asleep I dream of insomnia and wake up exhausted! The only known cure I have found is the realization at 5 a.m. that I have to wake up in an hour and start getting ready for work….out like a light every time! I fall back asleep thus oversleeping till 8 a.m. whereby I have to play the popular morning game of "Mad Dash to make the kid's school bus". This fun-filled activity is followed by the life risking, "Let's see if I can corner my momma mini-van on two wheels at 75mph around the Shawangunk Mountains to beat my boss to work" Challenge.

I'm sure if I cut out all the caffeine, family stress, the hundred things on my mental 'to do' list, and shot the dog next door, I might be okay - but what fun would that be? I tried sleep aids but all I can say is that you better be lying down when you take one because like an "off" switch you will collapse mid-sentence over a plate of pasta. You will sleep for a week straight until someone yells in your ear with a microphone, "You just won the lottery." That will just make you cranky for sure… not only were you yanked out of a good dream about Brad Pitt but someone lied about a chunk of lottery money to boot. No amount of Paxil, Celexa, Prozac, St. John's Wort or any other concoction is gonna make me a functioning human after that happens.

I sarcastically sing along with the lyrics of the Rolling Stones, "She goes running for the shelter of her mother's little helper", take a good shot of espresso, and pray that the edge will be taken off THAT day. It's sad when you look at the clock at 9 a.m. and realize the whole day is just shot and you're already trying to figure out how you're gonna make it to the bedtime that just isn't gonna happen anyways.

So like any good person trying to find a resolution I consult a girlfriend that seems well-rested enough on some "sound" advice (Ugh. I'm so punchy I'm making bad puns now).

"Have you tried a glass of milk?" she says.

"I drink so much milk I should buy my own cow and hook her up out back with a sippy straw. I accidentally "moo" once in awhile."

"What about turkey meat — they say it puts you right out," she continues.

"Don't tease me," I retort.

"What about sex — that always works for me and my husband," she laughs.

"I'm separated, middle-aged, and have pre-schoolers that wake me up by climbing into bed and sticking their smelly feet up my nose. The most action I'm seeing these days is from fat old coots on 'psychotic-singles.com' asking if I'm on their menu that night — which is sooooo not happening."

"How about exercise? Do a few minutes on the treadmill and that will tire you out," she suggests.

"Great, so not only do I have a sleep disorder but now I'm Jenny Craig at 4 a.m., as well." I call her a sadist and click the off button to the phone while she's mid-sentence. That's how cranky you can get when you're sleep deprived.

Sleep is a precious commodity among humans. We crave it all the time and no matter how much you get you always feel like it's never enough when that buzzer goes off in the mornin'. You bargain with yourself, "Five more minutes and I swear I'll get up," knowing full well you're lying to yourself. If you don't get enough sleep most people tend to get a bit cranky and then spread their little "crap on a cracker mood" to everyone they meet during their day. I can't tell you how many times I ripped somebody's head off in the morning because it was just too damn early for any human to be awake and I didn't have my coffee yet.

If you're a night person you typically won't mesh well with a "morning" person. One jumps outta bed like a flippin' pop tart ready to start their day singing a bad "Annie" rendition of the sun and how it's gonna come up tomorrow. On the flip side the night person is just getting home with their clothes on backwards, climbing into bed with a hang-over, and flippin' you the bird for kicking it up a notch with your little Broadway parade of goody gumdrops.

We always push it staying up too late to watch some stupid TV show afraid we'll miss something. Many times you wind up working late on something that got pushed to the last minute whether it's a contract for a client or cupcakes for the school play. The sleep we always desire takes a back seat to everything and then when we need it the most it eludes us like a spiteful child. Suddenly you have insomnia, somebody is snoring, the dog won't stop chasing a rabbit in its dreams, or the amorous couple in the next apartment are havin' a marathon of a night.

Isn't it the worst thing when you have to put up with someone that snores, talks, farts, sweats, drools, sleep walks, screams, kicks or bites in their sleep? Does your husband snore so loud you're afraid he's gonna suck the paint off the walls on the inhale? Does your college roommate talk so much in his sleep you decide to get even by posting it on YouTube? Are you getting sick of the Menopause Fairy making you drench the bed in sweat each night creating a cold clammy waterbed you didn't ask for? Do you have a spouse that's kicking you to death with restless leg syndrome and you start kicking back just for spite? How many times has your nightmare-prone wife shocked you awake letting out a blood curdling scream that nearly gave you a heart attack? Let's not forget Grandma down the hall lettin' the worst gas possible rip a hole in the ozone and makin' the dog howl half the night. You start to wonder how the hell you get any sleep at all!

If you've ever had to deal with a person that snores you've probably insisted they try every stupid contraption on the market from goats milk to sleeping pills and even a piece of tape you stick on their nose which is so unattractive it kills your libido to boot.

People that talk in their sleep at least keep you entertained. If they're gonna keep you awake half the night you might as well have fun asking them questions like if your brother-in-law's havin' an affair or where Grandpa's fortune is hidden.

If you have chronic insomnia everything is upside down. You don't sleep right, poop right, eat right, everyone else in the house is asleep, and you're going broke from all the crap you're buying on QVC at 3 a.m. Unfortunately the people that have to put up with insomniacs get woken up out of a sound sleep by their loved one vacuuming at midnight, hammering somethin', or clinking around the kitchen looking for God only knows what. If Papa can't sleep ain't nobody gonna sleep.

Since the beginning of time people have been doing anything to get a good night's sleep. "Hey, Adam, what's that you're drinking?" "Funny you should ask, Eve. It's something I'm gonna call Nyquil to knock me the !@#$% out because I can't put up with you yappin' in your sleep night after night about some apple pie you're gonna bake me."

Talking, walking and eating (all at the same time while still asleep) is a tough one to deal with. There are people out there that have this problem. Believe me — I know! It's when... at any moment... say around 3 a.m... your man suddenly sleepwalks to the kitchen, eats a bowl of fruit loops... leaving half of it on the floor, before coming back to bed and waking you up to tell you, "Ya' know, you need to go on a diet. Oh...and the kids keep spilling fruit loops on the floor." *Oh... yeah... Definitely my favorite.* APPARENTLY the people that have this disorder do all this while completely asleep and have no knowledge of it occurring when they wake up the next morning.... Or at least that's their story and their stickin' to it for fear of the glaring eye of their woman scorned with a hot tweet at her fingertips.

So if you differ in your sleep habits with others that share your abode chances are the inevitable will happen…gasp… don't say it …twin beds or worse — separate rooms! Damn … time to invest in a crap load of Ambien!

~ "I DON'T HAVE TIME TO BE SICK." ~

How many times have we said to ourselves, "I don't have time to be sick"? Of course we don't have time to be sick. It's not like we look at our calendar and pencil it in like a vacation and say, "Oh, look, I have some free time the third week of September — I think I'll catch a whopping virus that week and dine on nothing but Jell-O, saltines, and ginger- ale. Woo Hoo!"

It always happens at the most inconvenient time when you just can't get to the doctor because you have too much going on. Take, for instance, my recent bout with a nasty ear infection. Trying to get one last swim in before the cold weather hit, I did a few laps in the family swamp — I mean "pool" — in an effort to stay slim.

"It's just like swimming in a lake," I reasoned with myself. Henceforth, I developed an infection that pounded like a crazed teenaged marching band. What to do? I didn't have the precious time to sit in a doctor's office waiting for some antibiotics and wondering why I didn't just order them from an online Mexican pharmacy that probably filled the capsules with Kool-Aid anyway. So I did the next best thing: hit up mom's pharmacy. Growing up, my mother had a purse stuffed with every drug you could need.

"Constipated? Here I got an enema — bend over."

"Pneumonia? Let me get my purse."

"Impacted tooth? I got Vicodin."

My mother was to medication like a squirrel was to nuts, stored for the winter. If someone didn't finish a prescription, it got nestled away for future emergencies. So I approached my mother with my malady as she was sitting with her cousins chatting away. "Where's your stash, Mom? I have an ear infection."

"Oh, I don't do that anymore - got rid of everything. I've gone all natural now," she said.

"What are all these bottles of pills in all these jars then?" I ask.

"Those are vitamins. Your cousin takes over a 100 different vitamins a day and keeps them in jars and swallows them at each meal by the jar-ful." The funny thing is that out of all of us, *she's* the one that gets sick the most - go figure.

So then my cousin chimes in: "Here, Carol, stick this clove of garlic in your ear. It's a natural antibiotic and will clear that up in no time," she says. Now, knowing the prankster nature of this wino brood, I hesitate, thinking that I will be the butt of some AARP joke. Reluctantly, I allow this odd remedy to take place, which resulted in odd cravings for Italian dishes and people in public sniffing at me oddly and thinking I had a fear of vampires.

So after a week and a flippin' pound of garlic I finally broke down and went to the walk-in clinic. After semi-hearing the doc's speech on the middle ear versus the outer ear type of infections (all that garlic made me deaf I think), I *finally* got a script for antibiotics. For the heck of it, that sweet, sweet man threw in some Vicodin. So then the next morning I woke up, popped one of each, and went to work hoping this would finally be resolved. Now if any of you called the office and talked to me that day, I sure as heck sounded like a complete idiot. My boss came in and I was all "Lucy in the Sky with Diamonds" spaced out. *Oy!*

So the lesson here, kids? If you're sick, stay home and take care of yourself the best way you can and all will once again go back to normal thereafter.... hopefully.

~ VIDAL SASSOON IS A FUCKIN' LIAR ~

Let's face it — we all age — we all turn gray. The vanity in us tries to fight the inevitable and in an effort to stay young we turn to our good friend, "hair dye." When I have a special event coming up I'll fork over the cash for a professional job but in the meantime, for touch ups, I go with Lady Clairol even though the color on the side of the box never seems to be the color it comes out. Sometimes it takes 2-3 times to get it right and by then your hair is burnt to a crisp and could pass for straw.

My grandmother has had her share of mishaps in this area. One time my brother brought his girlfriend home to meet the family on a Friday night for dinner. Grandma had just finished dying her hair but it must have gone bad because it came out green. The girl was a little wide-eyed but was polite. The next day we went to a big family picnic and the girlfriend saw Grandma was now a brunette. You'd think this was the end of it but apparently Grandma was still not satisfied with being a brunette either. She goes for round three and dyes it yet again to a light blonde. So you can imagine the look on the girlfriend's face by church on Sunday as yet a third look is revealed by Grandma. I'm equally surprised she wasn't bald by Sunday after three dye jobs in three days. The hair was still there but unfortunately spiked straight up to the moon resembling boxing promoter, Don King.

I have to say though, that Lady Clairol saved my butt when I was out in L.A. My sister took me to this famous hair dresser, "Pierre", that does the likes of Heather Locklear and Lindsay Lohan. I explained to the guy that I wanted blonde highlights but with one thin streak of red in the front. My sister went next door for a croissant and coffee and by the time she came back the job was just about done. I stared at the train wreck in the mirror with the whole front of my head dyed to a bright fuchsia. I looked like a troll doll!! My sister spit out her croissant in little chunks all over this hot pink horror show. "I can't let you leave looking like that," she hysterically laughed. She tells Pierre it looks horrible which offends him and he wasn't so gentle during the second dying. The end result was a disaster to say the least with me and my sister in tears. On the way home we stopped at Rite-Aid and got a box of Lady Clairol doing it a third time that night. It came out exactly how I tried to explain it to Pierre and it only cost $6 bucks! That and the $200 I blew at Pierre's' made it a total of $206 bucks. Oy!

Now taking care of one's hair after all this dying is a whole other kick in the can. I have found that the majority of shampoo and conditioner products are liars. Vidal Sassoon? With curly hair using his stuff I look like I've been through a tornado. I look more like Vidal "Monsoon" did my hair. I recently got taken in by the Garnier commercials with Sarah Jessica Parker promising me luxurious locks. She swore on national television that this product would cure my "fly away frizz." Well I couldn't get a comb through it. I broke the handle right off the brush fighting to get it through what had turned into a brillo pad on my head. So now I'm stuck with a whole bottle of both shampoo and conditioner of a product that is making me look like Little Richard. The dog didn't even like it when I tried the stuff on him. He went from looking like a collie to a poodle. Another lesson I've learned is no matter how enticing it looks don't ever buy shampoo and conditioner from the dollar store. There are a list of reasons why it's in the dollar store. You'll be riding the S.S. Baldy cruise on a journey to "all-your-hair-falling-out-in-clumps" land. It's not a happy place.

I honestly don't think there's a product alive that could tame my mane. A little girl told me last Halloween that I should go as a witch since I already have the hair for it. No matter what I do I always look like I just crawled out of a ditch after a night in the county lock-up. Too bad "electrocution" wasn't a popular look these days — I'd be a trendsetter. At least in the 80's I fit in with that "big hair" trend. I can't imagine why God thought this was a good look for me. Clearly we can rule God out as being skilled in the beautician career category. That could be a slogan for the hair styling industry: "God is not a beautician that's why he made hair stylists."

So I'm just going to accept that I'm going through life looking like witchy-poo. I told my friend Karla, that I was finally just gonna go natural and say to hell with it and turn gray already. She laughed and smirked, turning her eyes to her crotch while pointing, "Wait till it ALL goes white. Being a black woman I have to deal with a white streak down the middle and it makes me look like a skunk, so stop complainin' ya silly little white girl." An atomic mushroom cloud went off in my head at the unthinkable. Oh, Hell no. I just about got a ticket screeching to a halt at Rite-Aid in search of my best friend, Miss Clairol.

~ HAIRDO BY EDWARD SCISSORHANDS ~

Who, in this world, hasn't endured growing out a horrible haircut? How many times have you left from the salon crying in a hysterical rage that you were gonna sue the place? When arriving home from your recent appointment have others winced at the sight of you gasping, "Who the hell did your hair, Edward Scissorhands?" Yup - been there.

The older you get, the less you care — you're just happy ya' still have some on your head so you're not mistaken for your bald husband. A totally bizarre, messed up cut when you're young, however, could be devastating to whatever pathetic social life you've vainly tried to establish. I can't tell you how many scissor-happy hairdressers have completely butchered my locks over the years. I still get a knot in my throat thinking about the mishap I've labeled "the Troll Doll Incident" I might have mentioned. The horror!

My bad haircut days started in Kindergarten when my older brother suddenly decided he wanted to be a barber when he grew up. Since he'd already cut all the hair off all my Barbie dolls, I was the only one left to experiment on. He did the ultimate 'no-no' of running around the house with the biggest pair of sheers in hot pursuit of my head. When I finally ran out of breath and succumbed to his cutting obsession he took every last hair off my head — completely bald. Needless to say he didn't grow up to be a barber but instead became a rocket scientist for NASA, which is odd considering it's usually the opposite with little boys. They say they want to be a rocket scientist and wind up as a barber instead.

Ever since that bad haircut I've found it hard to really commit to one hairdresser. I try one out, get disappointed, and just move on to the next. I think I've been to every shop in the northeast and will have to start on the west coast now. In frustration I actually took a class so I could learn to cut my own hair. Unfortunately I can never see the back and it always looks like somebody did it and ran.

I don't even trust anyone cutting my own children's hair so I trim theirs as well. I figure why spend twenty bucks for someone to make my kid look like an idiot when I can do it for free. My girlfriend just raises her brow at me when she see's my little guy's Buster Brown bowl cut though. As a result she insisted she was taking him to a barbershop this week so the other kids wouldn't make fun of him. I finally caved and said I'd take him. "No, let me take him, I want to do it," she begged. After much prodding her ulterior motive was revealed: she actually had a crush on the shop owner and wanted to borrow my kid for an excuse to go in there. "You want me to pimp out my kid so you can get a date?!" I sneered. "Yeah, pretty much," she says. I was actually impressed by her new innovative man hunting technique and being I'm also a single mother in the pathetic dating pool I agreed out of curiosity.

What I neglected to tell her is that he doesn't like to get his hair cut and hysterically freaks out when he hears the buzz of the shears. When I try it myself, it's like a wrestling match trying to hold him down and not cut an ear off with both of us sweatin' bullets and growling at each other. This was sure to be entertaining to watch, so I sat outside and laughed at the forthcoming fiasco until a lollipop finally settled him down. She came out with a scowl and just glared at me. "What? No date?" I chuckle. Best money I ever spent on a bad haircut.

~ BLIND AS A BAT WITH
READING GLASSES ~

Getting old has its good points and bad points. You're finally past the emotional roller coaster of your 20's and 30's, obsessing over zits, the opposite sex, climbing the corporate ladder, getting married, and having babies. Now that you are a little older and actually know a few things, roll with the punches better, appreciate the little things more and perhaps achieved some goals, you think it's smooth sailing, and you can finally getting around to doing some things you've always wanted to do.

Now the bad part. The spirit may be willing but the flesh is weak. You're ready to use your wisdom and experience but now your various body parts declare mutiny and start falling apart. Your 20,000 mile warranty just expired on your chassis and now you need a new kidney, or rotator cuff, and it's hard to get good parts these days unless they're made from a pig gut or cow spleen.

Lately with me it's been my "bad eyesight" changing from "bad" to downright "gangsta' nasty bad." My eyes are so bad even laser surgery wouldn't help and they turned me down. The lenses on my glasses are so thick that if I wear them for an hour I get a migraine from the weight on my face practically tipping me over. So basically I've been wearing contacts since they were invented. Unfortunately, I started to notice that even with the right contact prescription I can't see close up to read a book, take out a splinter, or write out a birthday card. When I was at a restaurant last week and pulled out my kid's bug magnifying glass to read the menu, my girlfriend says, "Oh hell no you are NOT gettin' all Grandma on me and reading the menu with that thing." I guess if you're out cruisin' for a nice divorcee it doesn't look all that smokin' hot to be pullin' out a device that could be used to see amoebas.

So I figured it was about time to make the yearly trip to the eye doctor. The doctor suggested I try wearing one contact that allows me to see things far away, and then the other contact would let me see things close up. Sounded kinda' cockamamy to me but he's the one with the degree on the wall so I decided to give it a go for the two weeks he suggested. Apparently somehow that would allow my brain enough time to adjust and make it all come together.

Well, let me tell ya' the world started lookin' pretty twisted for a while; like I was in a 3-D movie and walking on marshmallows at the same time. At least I'd have an excuse if I run over my neighbor's dog that barks all night. "Sorry, Mr. Smith, I got these new contacts in and I didn't even see your Great Dane lunging for my car." I found myself closing one eye to read the road signs hoping not to drive off the bridge, and the other eye to read the recipe for dinner hoping not to put oregano in the pie and cinnamon in the sauce. Being out in public blinking one eye closed to see the ladies room door or other eye to see the contents of a cereal box got strangers thinking I was winking at them. A guy in his 70's at the supermarket whistled back, "Ya ain't so bad yourself there, girlie." I finally put on my son's pirate eye patch to make things easier but it just gave me an uncontrollable urge to say things like, "arrghh… ya scurvy dogs."

I finally went back to the doctor and said I just couldn't do it. So the last resort was to wear the same contacts I had been wearing which would enable me to walk around and not bump into walls, and to go to Rite-Aid for a $5 pair of reading glasses to put over the contacts when I want to see close up to read. Sigh… kinda' defeats the purpose of having the contacts but the only other option would be to strap on a couple of magnifying glasses to me face, I suppose.

So what will be next? My hearing? My toes? My teeth? I should borrow Vanna's wheel of fortune, write my body parts on it and take bets. "Carol spins the wheel … where will it land, folks? What area of her body will need fixin' next? She puts her money on bursitis….oh, just misses and lands on a colonoscopy…. Aww… tough break!" So it goes…

~ CHANGING THE WORLD ONE SHOWER AT A TIME....~

There's nothing like waking up on a Saturday morning and being able to finally take a long hot shower and let out a big sigh that you don't have to go 90mph in a mad dash to make work and the school bus.

During the week your shower is rushed while screaming through the door at your children to stop fighting and finish their breakfast. You have about three minutes for this shower because everyone else made you late. Shaving your legs is like chopping down trees with a butter knife because it's been a while and you have to wear a dress for that big meeting. Unfortunately in your mad rush your legs wind up a bloody mess. You can't slow down and appreciate those designer shower gels in the cute little bottles that you got at that cute country store in Vermont. So they sit unused, unloved, gathering soap scum waiting for a Saturday to be appreciated.

Why is it that whenever you want to get into the shower someone's always gotta run the dishwasher or washing machine? No water pressure and the whole thing is shooting out ice-cycles! And why is it that someone always has to use the toilet when you're in there? It's just so wrong! All these people are the same ones that load up the shower stall with a zillion bottles of shampoo or conditioner all with only a drop left in them. And then when you want to shampoo your hair there's not one bottle to be found but there's eight bottles of conditioner. Then to make matters worse all the manufacturers make the words so small you can't tell which one is the conditioner and which one is the shampoo. Why can't they be like the salt and pepper shakers and put a big ol' "S" or "C" on them? I can't tell you how many times I thought I was putting shampoo on and it was conditioner.

Face it, next to the kitchen the bathroom is the most important room in the house. When you are in the market to buy a house one of the first things you do is check out the bathroom. If you're as anal as I am (no pun intended) you just gotta know that the shower is going to meet your standards. A good shower can soothe your soul after a long hard work week, make your aches go away, comfort you in times of sorrow when you just found out someone died, resolve conflicts as you do your best thinking in there, invigorate you after a great work out and is a good substitute for a husband when you hit a rough patch (admit it — hand held shower heads are truly an ingenious invention keeping miserable housewives happy everywhere). It's your best friend. No one knows you like your shower. Like Bogie says, "This is the beginning of a beautiful friendship".

I've yet to find the bathroom of my dreams though. I have a fantasy that one day I'd go house hunting and happen upon the most glorious mother of all bathrooms and suddenly hoards of angels appear blaring heavenly trumpets: DUN-DUN-DUNNNNNN! In my dreams the shower is a walk-in with glass doors, has about eight jets that shoot from all over and a built-in seat so I can sit my lazy ass down. Magical shower fairies at night would clean and continually re-stock it with every kind of wonderful scented, lathery, heavenly products all for my showering pleasure. Wouldn't that be great?! Unfortunately for the time being my only option would be to hook up the kid's Elmo sprinkler to the shower head and put the plastic lawn chair in there — closest thing to a spa I'm gonna get right now.

I think my obsession all began with that commercial from the seventies with the woman getting all excited about her bath crystals, "Calgon, take me awaaaaaaayyy!" she'd sigh into the camera. A good product can do that I will admit. God help the child in my household that messes with my soap. I have recently admitted that I am completely addicted to homemade lilac soap. I'm spoiled now and no other commercial soap will do. I can see myself eventually having to go to a Soap Anonymous meeting. "Hello. My name is Carol and I have a soap addiction that is leading to a massive water bill and pruney skin."

When I was a young girl my sister and I were at my cousin's fifth birthday party and went to use the bathroom there. Some eighteen year old slutty family friend was visiting and came out of the bathroom from her shower and being a real smart-ass inappropriately exclaimed to a room full of our elders that, "Showers are better than sex!" Everyone was stunned into silence and the kid's mother dropped the birthday cake on the floor out of shock. It always stuck with me. Makes me wonder how many hand held shower heads that chick has gone through by now.

~ CHAPTER SIX ~

THE DAILY GRIND

Life wouldn't be complete if other people, besides our families, annoyed us to no end within the daily grind of each day. What would we do with ourselves if we didn't have to deal with the DMV, traffic tickets, junk mail, or bad interviews? Hmm…. probably be much happier.

Too bad I can't wave my magic wand and make all the following annoyances disappear….

~ WHAT'S WITH ALL THE COPS LATELY? ~

Is it me or have the cops been a bit overkill lately on our local roadways? I travel around quite a bit and usually go decades without a ticket but lately they're all over the place ticketing all the locals just trying to make a living. Now I know they need our dollars to support the municipal troll under the bridge, but I just got a ticket for not using my left blinker (being in the left hand turning lane at a light is usually a good heads up to the other drivers that you are turning left). C'mon!!

God forbid, there's actually a bank robbery because they'll be too busy giving some poor handicapped person a ticket for having an air freshener hanging from their rear view mirror. "Sir, put your hands up on the wheel where I can see them!" "What did I do, officer?" "You have a Patriots air freshener tampering with your ability to see the road clearly, and since it's not the Jets I'm giving you a second fine."

I just got done going to court for a speeding ticket in a little village in upstate New York. The whole village is 30mph except one little itsy bitsy block that is sneakily 20mph — just one block — then back to 30mph all around. So, of course, the fuzz likes to sit on this one block waiting for good unsuspecting people to make their ticket quota and squeeze every last dime out of us. We are then forced to live off of peanut butter and hot dogs for the next month. I was one of those unfortunate people that got snagged on this ridiculous block and now my children are having nightmares from it. I was "speeding" at a wild whopping, nail-biting 28mph. They're both crying like they've been stabbed. "Are you going to jail, Mommy?" "Please, Mr. Policeman don't take my mommy away and put her in prison." So now my children are scarred for life thinking I'm going to the big house and the cop is asking me where I'm going now.

Why is it they always gotta ask where you've come from and where you're going and why you're speeding. Even if you have the most valid reason in the world it really doesn't matter. Case in point: when I was nine months pregnant with my son and was traveling on Route 84 when I started not feeling so well. I only had another twenty miles to go, I was in a desolate part of the highway, I didn't own a cell phone at the time and suddenly I think I'm in labor. (I know everyone just cringed not because I was in labor but at the horror of not owning a cell phone). I start speeding up because I didn't want to be stuck on the side of the road popping out my little boo and not be able to call for help. So I get pulled over by deputy dog and without even letting me say a word he starts yelling at me about how fast I was going and where's the fire and yadda yadda as I'm doing my Lamaze breathing. After seeing all those cop shows where people try to explain themselves and they wind up in a choke hold in the back of the squad car, I decided to just let him rant, take my ticket and go. I assumed when I explained myself to the judge he'd understand. Nope. Holding my infant in the loaded court room he grilled me. "If you were in labor why didn't you ask the officer for assistance?" "He was mean and yelling - I couldn't get a word in edge-wise especially since I was hyperventilating and quite honestly explaining that I just lost my mucous plug was not on the agenda at the time." "A what plug?" he says. "Listen, your honor, I haven't had a ticket in ten years, so I'm not a habitual law breaker and obviously not a felon, I was in fact in labor because I'm standing here with my screaming newborn so if there was ever a valid reason to speed to one's location this would be it so could you dismiss the case?" He slapped me with a three hundred dollar fine which I had to pay IN CASH right there, and was told if I sped through New York again in the next three years he'd take my license away for good. Can you believe that?! Its reasons like this I have problems with our justice system – there obviously isn't one.

I gotta watch my back now. Writing about the "law" doesn't tend you get you a warm pat on the back....unless they're putting you in handcuffs for writing a humor column about them that they didn't think was all that funny. Watch, I'll get a ticket for jay walking to the deli for lunch this week. You know, if it weren't for a hardened criminal such as myself, taking all the police attention, rampant amounts of heroin wouldn't make it to their destinations and the dealers would all be out of business.

~ "STICK 'EM UP, LADY!" ~

So there's been a rash of burglaries on my street recently, it appears. You can't even call where I live a "neighborhood" because that would require neighbors… well… human ones at least. I don't think I can count the bears as neighbors. I live on a dirt road in the middle of alien abduction territory, miles away from civilization. I don't know about you but if I were a thief I'd stick to places in the city simply because it's more convenient. What idiot would want to drive out into the middle of East Cow Pie-ville for a lousy TV set? The hassle of going so far out in the wilderness would seem like too much effort for those with criminal tendencies. Besides… they'd get lost in all the back roads. "Hey Louie, didn't we make a left at that last big rock or was it a right at that old tree?" "Hell, I don't know, Max, it's not like there's a boy scout with a compass on every corner out here — we should have stolen a GPS!"

Quite honestly, if anyone broke into my house they would probably take pity on me and leave a couple of twenties on the kitchen table. That would be the kitchen table with only three legs next to the one rickety chair that hasn't broken yet. They'd leave the TV since they wouldn't know what to make of the two metal sticks pokin' outta' the top. Those would be antennae, boys, from back in the dark ages when TV was first invented and had knobs to turn the channel to one of only five stations. From that room they'd see the first computer invented in my bedroom. I'm pretty sure it was Steven Jobs' first attempt at a PC since it's made out of milk cartons, duct tape, and powered by squirrels constantly threatening to go on strike if they don't get more nuts. Stereo? Hell no — I got a turn table with a crank that still plays 45's. The squirrels like to mess with me and put the speed up to 33 rpm's so it sounds like their chipmunk cousins Alvin, Simon and Theodore. If you're under the age of twenty-five you have no idea what I'm talking about and you probably just hurt your brain trying to figure out what 33 rpm is. If you tried looking it up on Wikipedia you probably got a response of, "Your guess is as good as mine, Dude." Now the older generation is cursing me out thinking, "What the hell is Wikipedia?"

So I have no fear that if anyone broke into my house to steal anything they'd walk out empty handed and hysterically laughing. "Well, they could steal your identity though," my mother says. "Who the hell would want to be ME?!" I retort. I don't even want to be me some days! "They could take your checks and cash them all over town," she argues. I laughed myself into a case of the hiccups over that remark thinking about the $15.32 I have left in there till payday. Besides, everyone knows me as that "Smirk" chick so if they tried to pass themselves off as me they'd probably get a belt in the mouth for something I wrote. They wouldn't even get far with my ID since my credit score is minus ten. It's shot from defaulted student loans in the 90's because I decided to "eat" instead of trying to pay back the government for a degree that was supposed to get me a good job. Those commercials saying, "Go back to school and get your degree" never tell ya' you'll be living off of Spaghetti-O's for a decade because the economy tanked and now you're enslaved to somebody named "Fannie Mae" to buy back your soul to the tune of $50,000.

Yeah, that little bitter reality pill just made every thief in the tri-state area think, "Yeah, I think we should skip this chick's house... she's nuts…her friend Fannie is puttin' the squeeze on 'er, she's got a rodent problem, and she just might blow our heads off over some European TV with metal sticks that she seems very attached to." That's right, guys, you just keep driving past my house and save yourself a whole mess of problems.

~ D.M.V. =
DASTARDLY MORONIC VULTURES ~

Me and the D.M.V. **do not** see eye to eye let me tell ya'. No matter how well prepared you are it's always something that isn't right or some paper you forgot and you have to drive the forty-five minutes back another day. They're never open on Saturdays, and only one day of the week is designated as a "late day" when they're open after 5 p.m. Never mind the rest of the world works all day and can't get there before closing. I swear they're in cahoots with the post office, they're illegitimate cousin — yet another organization that won't stay open after 5 p.m., really screwing anyone that has a PO Box since they can't get their mail.

My most recent bout with the Department of Motor Vehicles was trying to switch my Driver's License from my former home in Connecticut to my current home in New York. Yeah…yeah… I know you have to change it a month after you move but I'm a little over a few months… or years… So I finally schlepped my cookies all the way to that building of red-taped hell with it's vulturous minions to sit and wait an eternity for my number to be called. Now this is the second time in two weeks that I've had to do this since the first try I didn't have my birth certificate. I gave them eight other pieces of photo ID but they needed *that* one. So here I was once again poking the bear and hoping for some honey.

Things were going smoothly at first. I pulled everything out of my big ol' mama purse like Mary Poppins pulling out a coat rack. She asked me for everything under the sun from my debit card (odd request — hope she didn't go buy something online when she was gone for 20 minutes with it), a utility bill, pay stub (another odd request), my old license, any former NY licenses I had, and my birth certificate. I handed her a large envelope containing my birth certificate and she gasped when she saw it. The poor little thing was worn, ripped, taped up, and as holey as swiss cheese. "Wow, this is old," she said absentmindedly, debating whether she should accept it like she was the elderly license police. I raised a brow and tartly replied, "Yeah, I should probably put it in a glass case before it disintegrates… but, hey, don't I look good for a 105 years old?" After scrutinizing it for a long time she finally accepted it, took my mug shot, charged me the $55.00 highway robbery fee, and just as she was about to complete everything she asks if I've ever had a license in NY before. Damn it, I should have said "no". Apparently they wanted to give me back the same number I had but they had me in their computer system as having one in each name — both the married and maiden names. So their "system" couldn't converge them and they had to send some form up to Albany which is gonna take forever …. "You mean I have to come back a third time to get this damn license?" Now you could almost see the exclamation points coming out of my head and smoke coming out of my ears. I couldn't believe it. I gave her every document she wanted, paid my fee and because of a glitch in their stupid system I had to do it all over again thereby wasting yet another two hours of my life for a third week in a row.

As she goes to get her manager I look down at the row of windows along the counter and to see other people begging the DMV agents to fulfill their requests as well. God it was so pathetic! The poor college kid at the end shockingly argued, "What do you mean you're taking away my license because I was six months late on my car insurance? I can't drive at all? I can't just pay a fee? How am I gonna get to work?" Then there was this poor slob trying to register his boat getting all bent out of shape when they said his former registration was missing a few digits, "But that's the only registration it's had and if you registered it before with a few missing digits it's obviously possible to register now!"

I just shook my head and burst out laughing at the craziness of it all. No wonder they have a cop sitting there at the end of the counter. I wonder what the statistics are for how many times a week someone dives over the counter trying to choke the attendant. Maybe that's why the county jail is in the same building — the cells are filled with people that had melt-downs when they heard, "It's the system."

Damn, wouldn't you know it but that was the *one* driver's license photograph that came out good too!!!!

~ "THE CAR BROKE DOWN!" ~

No matter how old you get you worry about your kids when they get behind the wheel. You're practically middle-aged and your retired mother will still say, "Call me when you get home — ring the phone once and I'll know you got home okay." The most dreaded phone call you can get is your kid calling you in the middle of the night from a desolate highway an hour away saying those horrible four words that make you wince, "The car broke down." God, we've all been there and boy doesn't it suck?!

I've had the worst luck with my last few cars…not unlike my last few relationships… hmpft… cars and men always seem to give me trouble. With this particular car it had both strikes against it — it was a car I bought from my ex-boyfriend who my father couldn't stand — so it was the "bad-luck-mobile" in his eyes. The fact that it's a sporty devil red little number and I'm trying to break my addiction to speeding like a race car driver doesn't help either…it's a recipe for disaster. Funny…much like the relationship was.

So I took said car that I like to call, "Big Red" (because it sure likes to take me for a ride) and I stopped for gas and filled up the tank, rushing off to work. I didn't get even a mile down the road and the thing breaks down. Apparently the gas station's tanks were filled with water due to all the flooding and what was actually pumped into my tank was 90% water. Not something that typically happens to most people so of course it happens to ME. As a matter of fact it must be a new addition to God's little idea list of conflicts to throw at the humans. He seems to like to try out his brainy new "challenges" on me in particular. "Hey, St. Peter, watch this — I'm gonna snap my fingers and change gasoline to water and see how Carol deals with it." "Now Lord, you just got over testing her with that Chihuahua incident, the least you can do is let her break down right in front of an auto mechanic place."

Well luckily I did and they fixed my car up good as new and the gas station was covering the cost to fix it for putting the water in there in the first place…. but then I pressed my luck and tried to take a trip to the mall that night. Say you're driving down the highway when out of nowhere the engine light pops on and it just dies... shuts off… the bad part is that means the power steering is also gone and at 65mph in the left lane in the middle of passing a car your wheel is locked stiff. Yeah, that's a boatload of fun you can't get at Six Flags.

So get this crap — the needle was on the "F" and it was full and they told me they did put gas into the car — all seemed well. Suddenly it plummeted to "E" and it was empty. So now I'm out of gas, stuck at night, with my crying kids and the phone is dying. I got a call out to my parents for a half a second to say I was stuck and that was it. They were just served their dinner at their favorite restaurant and took one sip of wine before hearing "the car broke down". {{Sigh}} Whatcha' gonna do? Of course you're gonna take the meal to go and come to your middle aged black sheep daughter's help once again. So like the troopers my parents are they drove out to get me and got a tow truck as well.

In the meantime I was highly impressed by a kind stranger named Doug who stopped to help me. The poor man tried to help me get a gas can and some gas by looking around for a gas station but there was nothin' but mountains and Big Foot out there it seemed. God bless his heart for trying as hard as he did though. Every once in awhile I get surprised by someone that is kind enough to reach out and try to help another in need — that must'a been St. Peter's touch right there...

So what's the moral of this story? That God can change gas into water? I'm the village idiot for not keeping my cell phone charged? Strangers named Doug that drive pick-up's are a safe bet not to chop you up into little pieces? That Big Red is no more? That perhaps, I should have listened to my father and gotten rid of the car like I did the idiot ex-boyfriend? I think it means that no matter how old I get my parents will always come get me when cars and men give me trouble.

~ DEAR PEN PAL... ~

So I was watching a news program the other day that stated that since the written word has become obsolete with today's texting, keyboard-ish tendencies, the public schools are going to drop teaching cursive handwriting. They said it was no longer necessary and it will fade into the abyss of forgotten things. What a sad day!

Being a writer I truly love the beauty of cursive handwriting with its soft swooping curves, fragrant ink and gentle slant. It makes me long for the days of feather or quill-type fountain pens with ink in ornate inkwells. I always loved those big plume ink pens; so fancy and delightful; how could you not have a smile on your face writing with one of those? Each person's handwriting is also unique to only them — like your very own snowflake. No one else's is quite like yours, making it a very personal thing — can't get that from a text, or an email.

So this new hatin' of all things cursive will probably have a big effect on the art of letter writing; truly in danger so it seems. I'm so panicked about it I just want to go out and get a pen pal in the jungles of Guam who writes with squid ink on banana leaves and never heard of Facebook, or ...computers...

and maybe indoor plumbing… We could have great conversations about our different cultures, give the post office some business, and centuries from now people will find our letters and discover that cursive writing once existed. Now if I could only find some sort of store around here that still sells stationery (although they probably have dust on them) and maybe some real books that don't have to be downloaded. Lord!

My daughter is going into third grade next year and will be learning cursive writing unless they decide to make it optional now. I'd be nervous for her if they kept it because this year her report card was all good… *except handwriting*. It's all in her grip...she tends to hold it like she's going to go all Lizzie Borden on the paper, stabbing it with the pencil. Throws me back into my own third grade class in the dark ages and the stern eye of Mr. Carter trying to get me, a lefty, to slant to the right like the righties. He kept telling me to curl my hand around practically crippling myself; but I wouldn't do it. I tried to reason with him that it's more comfortable to slant to the left if you're a lefty and slant to the right if you're a righty. Made sense to me. He grew irate and yelled something about "How dare I question him" and called my parents in for a conference. All three of them sat my eight-year-old butt down to a "talkin' to" about the importance of good penmanship and how I'll never get anywhere in life if I can't write properly. I don't know how but I won that battle I think because they were so exasperated, and they let me slant to the left.

The fact that not a soul can read a thing I've written on paper but myself is not such a bad thing. It's like my own secret code. Unfortunately there have been times when I can't seem to crack the code and figure out what the hell I wrote either. It's okay though, when that happens, I know just what to do — I knock on my neighbor's door. "Yeah, hi there, Dr. Miller, sorry to wake you up so early, but can you read what I've written down here? I can't seem to figure it out and I know it's important and since you're a doctor that has really bad handwriting as well, I thought maybe you could take a stab at it." He didn't seem too happy with me just then because when he translated, "Eggs, milk, butter, and juice" it was through clenched teeth. I have a feeling he is not going to be helpful in translating my pen pal letters from Guam.

~ THE WORST INTERVIEW EVER ~

I ran into my friend Mark the other day at the coffee shop and he looked a wreck. He was getting ready to go to an interview and it's been awhile since he's had to go to one and as I remembered, he really sucked at interviews. He was lucky some corporation hired him out of college and he hasn't had to worry about going on any interviews for fifteen years. But alas, with the lousy economy he got laid off. So he's been out of work for six months and is so depressed he just lies around having many a "pajama day", watching nothin' but sports, eating poppy seed bagels and Yoo-Hoo's mixed with Coors. He wallowed in pity and filthy underwear for days on end putting a permanent butt print in the middle of the couch watching the entire Star Wars boxed DVD set he got one Christmas… for himself. This is kinda' how guys grieve, I think. Girls have been well known for crying over a tub of ice cream after a romantic break up so I guess this is the guy's equivalent to that.

Well, eventually Mark man'd up, put down the after-breakfast beer, changed his underwear, got his confidence back, and finally landed an interview. That's when I ran into him at the coffee shop, since it happened to be across from the place he was trying to get hired at. I assured him he'd do well and wished him luck. Chance had it I got busy on the computer and a couple hours later he was back at the shop again, stinking like sewage, bug-eyed, and lookin' like he was just abducted by aliens and probed for the last three hours. "Mark, what the hell happened? Did the interview go okay?" He barely rasped out in a bone dry, cracked whisper, "It……was……the…. worst….. interview………..E-V-E-R-R-R-R." I immediately started rummaging' in my purse for a valium, or a tranquilizer….somethin' … anythin'… a tic tac maybe ….to offer the poor slob. All I had was sticky Pez candy with fuzz on it I passed off as a Percocet and an elephant head finger puppet I tried to amuse him with to get him to blink and stop drooling.

Apparently, someone had told him that this company drug tested and that his six month depression of eating nothing but poppy seed bagels would somehow trigger the test into a false positive from the poppy seeds. Absolutely paranoid he goes to GNC in a state of panic screaming at the pimply faced teenager behind the counter, "Hey, I need this job, so don't be messin' with me, man! I know you got @#$% in here that can make my pee pass a test!!" like some deranged coke addict. So he takes this "detox" solution to clean out his system but unfortunately winds up with such a "doubling-over case of the runs" right smack in the middle of the interview. The HR Manager steps out for a minute and he "thinks" he can just let the unbearable gas eating up half his leg seep out in a "silently but deadly…" but accidentally got more than he bargained for. With that the woman comes back in, coughs, and informs him that he now has to take a test in the next room "which also happens to be next to the restroom in case you need to use it," she gasps. Needless to say he completely bombed the test as well, not being able to concentrate on any of the questions smelling like a barn. He ranted to me all flabbergasted, "I had no idea I was going to have to take a test on history and politics, for Pete's Sake! I thought I suddenly was auditioning to get on Jeopardy! Not only did I stink the place up but I have no idea what the United Nations does, who the President of Greece is, what happened in 1049 AD, or dates of the Korean War! When they asked who runs Tanzania all I could think of was to write that my girlfriend just loves Tanzanite jewelry. And the only person I knew on the famous list of people was Amy Winehouse only because that messed up English wench dropped dead recently. They could have at least made it multiple choice!" After his little meltdown sobbing over poppy seeds, pooped pants, and not knowing when Kennedy was shot, I assured him he still had a chance. "Mark, they are NOT posting your failed test on Facebook and laughing about the idiot that crapped in his pants!" He started to cheer up a bit and calm down. "I feel a little bit better now," he says. "It's probably that fuzzy Percocet finally kicking in I guess." {sigh} Yeah….he's soooo not gonna get that job.

~ THE JUNK MAIL MASSACRE ~

I don't know about you but if I get one more junk email about Viagra, a million dollar inheritance from someone in China, penis enlargement devices (like I need that?), or how to get cheap prescription drugs from Mexico I'm gonna take a hatchet to my computer. In the old days you just had to worry about getting your junk mail the old fashioned way in the mailbox but now it's just about everywhere it seems. I'm sure I'll be sitting on the commode one day and the thing will suddenly start playing the jingle for Charmin toilet paper. Geez! Back in the day it was Ed McMann and his Clearing House Sweepstakes clogging up the mailbox but now it's a whole other level of hell as they invade your computer. I feel like a frightened Dorothy in the Wizard of Oz but instead of singing "Lions and Tigers and Bears, Oh my" it's more like "Viruses, Pop-up's and Spam, Oh My!" There's just no end to this crap.

The fact that they even made up a new term for it: "Spam" kinda' says it all. I wonder if the makers of Spam meats are all bent about that term being coined for stuff you don't want. Although it makes sense — Spam meat is typically something I don't want either. Although it sells very well in Guam I hear. Not like I got an "in" on all the hot gossip going on in Guam or anything. "Hey Gertie, we better get down to the Guam Stop N' Go Mart — they're having a big blow out sale on Spam and I want to get in line before they sell out!" Ha!

When I think of the term "pop up's" it used to give me visions of pop tarts, donuts holes, jack-in-the-boxes — happy thoughts in general. Now in the age of electronics, pop-ups are horrible things like half naked women popping up on my screen asking me to chat with them. "Where's my powdered donut?!" I yell back at her. The only response I get is another pop-up telling me about all the singles in my area that are dying to meet me. Unfortunately the people they put in these pictures are nothing like the fruit loops that subscribe to these sites. Obviously false advertising there… and no donut to boot!! Then there are the ones telling me they found a miracle weight loss product that will make me a size zero in a week or can restore my hair to luxurious Rapunzel type locks or insist I need yet another odd kitchen gadget for a kajillion dollars. The only kitchen item I need is Alice from the Brady Bunch cookin' a feast for me every night for free and I don't see that happenin' in the forecast any time soon.

God, when I think about the crap I get on the computer AND in my mail box on a yearly basis it throws me into a panic attack remembering a fiasco years ago that can only be described as a junk mail massacre. One day I started receiving odd products in the mail that I had not ordered. So of course I tried to return the products but since I opened the box I had to pay to have it returned which was about $10 for each package! At first I thought it was an innocent mistake but then every day I came home to six or seven boxes on my doorstep. EVERY DAY!!! Piles of velvet paintings of Geronimo, Elvis plates, leprechaun statues, Playboy magazine subscriptions mixed in with Catholic Digest subscriptions (ain't that a hoot), just about anything from the Franklin Mint, commemorative coins, back scratchers with Betty Boop on them, garden gnome toe nail clippers…the list was endless. I tried to call the companies (not 800 numbers AND I was put on hold racking up a $50 phone call to Yemen no less) to ask how they got my contact information and to stop mailing me stuff. Apparently someone had it in for me and was pulling out all the postcard offers out of magazines and putting my name and address down, checking off "bill me". They had no way of tracing it either. The cops said they couldn't do anything since it wasn't a violent crime and told me to talk to the post office who said that although it's mail fraud they weren't able to trace it or figure out whose handwriting it was. There was literally nothing I could do but suffer through it. It went on for *6 months* with no end in sight!! Can you imagine?! 6 months! What a nightmare! I'm hyperventilating just thinking about it right now. I had no way of ending it and every day I had to spend my lunch hour going to the post office with boxes of crap since they don't fit into the mailbox and then I had to pay a huge phone bill from all the calls to stop the shipments. I started acting squirrelly, getting hives, and sinking into madness while developing an odd facial tick at the mere mention of Junk Mail!

I finally broke down in tears to my unemployed first husband at the time. Who could be so evil? What had I done to deserve this? That's when it suddenly stopped. Apparently he was having an affair with my best friend and they decided to have some "fun" with me. Isn't that just a kick in the head?! I hear they are happily living in Albany. Hmm… it's been about 12 years….maybe they wouldn't mind me sending them a couple of Elvis Plates for a few months. Ya think?! ~smirk~

~ "SOMEBODY PICK
UP THE PHONE!" ~

Who here hasn't tried to be on the phone having a conversation and immediately your children are at your feet screaming about something they need. "I can't even talk on the phone for five minutes without you kids going cuckoo bananas," I growl. "What could be so important? Is the house on fire? Are you trapped under a large rock? If you're not bleeding you're fine and it can wait till I'm off the phone!" I rarely get on the phone but it's amazing how they choose that exact moment to go completely crazy running around screaming their little heads off.

I actually hate talking on the phone to be honest, so when I'm on it's for something important. I think I have what I like to term, "phone anxiety". I fought getting a cell phone for the longest time but now that there's no such thing as pay phones anymore it's kinda necessary in case your car breaks down. I'd say E-mail and texting is my thing if I really have to contact someone – makes sense since I'm a writer I suppose.

I always give people my home phone number instead of my cell knowing full well I don't have an answering machine and I'm never home. But then when I'm home and the phone rings I don't answer it because if it's REALLY someone I want to talk to or desperately needs to get in touch with me they'd have my cell phone number. So that solves that problem. Then I put my cell phone on vibrate and that's my excuse for not hearing the cell ring. I know that's terrible, right?!

I think part of this phobia stems from my mother trying to make some extra money making a nickel per call doing telemarketing as a stay at home mom in the sixties. She was always on the phone and you couldn't get her attention. This is important if, say, your brother is chasing you around the house brandishing scissors in an attempt to start his kindergarten barber career. Unfortunately being on the phone with a client she couldn't yell but had to resort to wild hand gestures with gritted teeth and smoke comin' outta' her ears. Didn't stop my brother from making me as bald as a cue ball though. There wasn't even enough hair left for a barrette and I was forced to wear pink dresses till it grew back. No wonder I hate the telephone…. and pink dresses. Oh the years in therapy.

So it's a big step for me to have a cell phone these days although it's a basic flip model and my girlfriends make fun of me. "How's that Jitterbug 'ya got there? Get it from AARP magazine with an early bird coupon or something?" They flash their smartphones in front of me with all their slick, fast paced technology that is smarter than they are. "It can do practically anything" they boast. "Hey, when it can get up and make me a cup of coffee and pancakes then I'll consider buying one," I snarl back. As they continue to state their case about how 48% of all cell users now have a smartphone and how I need to get out of the dark ages, all I can picture in me head is a future society of people-droids that just plug *themselves* into a wall socket to re-charge.

It's amazing how the telephone was supposed to bring people together but instead it seems to have alienated people to the point that they don't know how to interact without it. I've actually seen people sitting in the same room and instead of talking to each other they're texting to each other. Have we become so socially numb that we can't talk to one another face to face anymore? Somewhere on a cloud looking down at us is Alexander Graham Bell shaking his head and thinking "What have I done?" Next to him is the father of the atom bomb saying, "You're preachin' to the choir there, Alex."

~ DON'T STEP ON MY BLUE SUEDE SHOES ~

Shoes. Now that's a hot topic… everyone needs them unless of course your job is to walk across coals in your bare feet in a third world country. Maybe that guy doesn't need them; but I think the rest of us could relate. So – here's my thing about shoes.

I have a beef with shoe makers – not the little cobblers of old that had elves help in the night but the mass market of big box store shoe supplier of women's and children's shoes. Men's shoes are all the same – nothing unique there to talk about – they're all flat and black or brown. Unless you're Elton John or Prince or "the Artist formerly known as Prince" that goes by a symbol (or is he back to Prince again?) well you know.

Shoe manufacturers make a killing just from children's shoes alone because they're always growing out of them quickly; it drives me nuts. The kids always need new shoes constantly because their damn feet won't stop growing. Every time I turn around one of them is complaining that their toes are all scrunched up and they're too tight. Because of this those shoe makers have us over a barrel and can charge ridiculous prices knowing full well we're gonna be back there again in a month forced to do it all over again.

And shoving your kid's foot into a pair of shoes will work up a sweat for sure. All over the kids department frustrated women are griping at their kids and pressing on the toe of the foot saying, "Is this where your toe is; where's your toe?" The ones that fit all our criteria never seem to come in their size. It's the outlandish shoes that are all sparkly in neon colors that nobody else wanted, that seem to be in her size. For my little guy nothing ever "feels good". As a matter of fact "It doesn't feel good" describes pretty much anything poor Buster Brown could throw at my son. My criteria for a shoe is that it's not gonna cost me an arm and a leg to buy the shoe and it's durable as hell because if they don't outgrow them in a month they'll be torn, tarred and missing a heel for sure. Not like any of this matters since they'll wear the shoes once, get a humongous blister that no band-aid can appease and they'll never be worn again. They have a whole closet full of those. It's all I can do but try to keep myself from driving past the Kinney Plant and whip a dozen of these blister shoes at them whilst yelling profanities of what they can do with their shoes.

Ahh… but my real dilemma with shoe makers is the women's shoes. It just chaps my hide that all the shoe stores start their women's shoes at a size 6; occasionally you can find a store that starts at a 5-1/2 but that's a rarity. I have a size 5 foot and it's a miracle if I go somewhere and find "one" pair of shoes – in any style – boot, flat, heel, sandal, doesn't matter – no-one ever has a size 5 of anything. When I come upon a new store and accidentally stumble upon a pair it's like finding a unicorn with wings in a traffic jam that magically lifts you out of the hell that is your life. Doesn't matter what it is either – even if it's a ghastly pair of red cowboy boots with green sparkly tassels – if it's a size 5, I'm buyin' it. God knows I'll never find another pair for miles… may be years before there's another sighting of this rare elusive creature.

I remember after college I had to go on all these interviews in my power suit and couldn't find not one pair of high heels in a size 5 and you just can't show up with a tailored skirt in sneakers. I remember being so exasperated at Payless Shoes that I had a meltdown on the store clerk about what the hell are short women supposed to do – just go barefoot? "Maam, I'm sure we can find something for you in the children's department," she said. I fought the urge to choke her to death. I can't believe she was suggesting I suffer the indignity of having to wear a pair of white patent leather Mary Jane's like I was a 9 year old going to Easter Mass, to a job interview at Pratt & Whitney Corporation as an Executive Department Head. So I had a bit of a meltdown that entertained my fellow mall shoppers and filed a complaint that they need to accommodate all their customers and not just the big foots of society and how I bet in China they don't have this problem since the average women's foot is a size 4. "See – the Chinese even beat the U.S. in accommodating small footed women," I scream like a lunatic at the clerk, leaving the store in an angry huff.

I get so jealous when I walk around seeing other women with these great new boots or heels in all shapes and colors and how much they just LOVE shoe shopping and have over two hundred pairs at home. I'm lucky if I can find one pair every three years to replace the one pair I had. When I do find a pair I wear it down to the nub until it's so worn out it's begging for mercy. It's really sad when a pair finally falls right off my feet like a broken horse that needs to be put down…. I almost feel like I need to honor them respectfully with a formal burial since they had to serve me for so long due to the shortage of their kind.

The only other issue I have with shoes is that the people that have no problem finding shoes would wear the right shoes for the right season. It's bad enough people can flaunt their various shoes all over the place but the least they can do is wear boots in the winter and flip-flops in the summer. I can't tell you how many times I've seen some teenage girl wearing a pair of suede boots roasting in the August heat of 98 degrees and some idiot college dude with unclipped toe nails wearing Birkenstock sandals in the snow like a moron.

Whew. Okay… got all that off my chest. Sorry about that… just continue to go about your day, my little meltdown is winding down now. Just gonna have a Xanax, lie down, and consider a new career as a barefoot coal walker in India.

THE FINALE
~ FRONT PORCH LIVING ~

Who doesn't love a porch on a beautiful day? With the tinkling of wind chimes, the creak of a rocking chair and chatter with loved ones as the sun begins to set;..... it provides a relaxation that soothes the soul just by sitting and thinking. As a child in the late afternoon heat of a summer's day, discussions with my Dad about triumphs and failures whittle away the hours. The women folk would either be snapping string beans from the garden into a colander or shucking corn for dinner on that worn and comfortable porch.

It seems that the porch is an important part of American culture. The front porch is where you go if two males in the family need to take it outside because of a heated discussion at the Thanksgiving table. The porch is where you get your first kiss when you get dropped off by your first crush on the best first date ever. Many a woman has been proposed to on her front porch. You might have even decided to take that new job on that porch. Parents have been told that they were going to be grandparents in nine months as they sat rocking in their favorite chair on the same porch they rocked their own babies.

You even got that scar on your knee from that porch when you rode your bicycle into it after taking off the training wheels.

One such memory of mine on the front porch involved my father and the first date I ever had. Now as a real young child my father told me that one day when I was a teenager he'd have to shoot the boys off the porch because I was so adorable. I honestly didn't think that was anything other than a cute, "Awww, Daddy" kinda moment but apparently he meant it.

I was with my first date, "Kevin", at the age of 16, who's older sister had to drive us to the movies as a chaperone just so I could go. Unfortunately we got a flat tire and it made me a half hour late for my 11pm curfew (all the teens out there are saying, "what's a curfew?" right about now). Unfortunately to make matters worse we couldn't call Dad to let him know of our delay because… hold onto your hats…. don't faint…. this was before cell phones were invented! GASP! The horror… I know! Back then there were things called "pay phones" – some of you kids might have heard of them or seen one in a museum. Well, there wasn't one in sight so I was basically screwed.

When we pulled up to the end of my very long driveway I told Kevin to pull over and say goodbye right there and I would walk the whole way up the driveway to face the music alone. Being a gentleman, he said he would walk me to the front door and simply explain what happened. Seeing my father on the front porch cleaning his rifle, I told him, "You don't understand - my father's gonna shoot you dead!" He tried to take it like a man but after my Dad said, "Carol Ann get in the house I want to have a talk with Junior here," I watched from the window as Kevin turned white as a sheet staring at my Dad's rifle. I never heard from him again after that. Maybe that's where all my dating troubles began --- with my father! Oy!

Another front porch moment of mine came when I sorta threw a party at my parent's house when they went away on vacation. Oh, c'mon, just about every teenager has thrown a party when they're parents were away – it's a rite of passage! Well, I was legal to drink at 19 years old and home from college and figured, "what the hell". Just about everyone in town was there and eventually the cops showed up which seems to be a requirement for all good parties. We were all on the front porch eating popcorn and enjoying the good fist fight going on in the front yard – hey it was free entrainment and every good party has a good fight anyways. One very young rookie cop asks two girls on the porch swing if they were legal to drink and they responded with something about their father being the town judge and all. He flippantly says, "Yeah, well, you might be appearin' in front of him tonight there, Missy!" all riled up. After that the Chief of Police was reprimanding his own son for smashing up my ATV on said lovely porch as the kid puked all over it. When the rest of the police looked around and saw all their teenaged kids were there and creating a nuisance with macaroni noodles on the ceiling and overflowing bubbles from the Jacuzzi creating massive damage, they got back into their cars saying, "Well, it looks like you have things under control here so just send our kids home in an hour and we'll consider the matter closed." The front porch suffered a permanent injury that night from all the ruckus but when I look at that missing chunk it makes me smile with a good memory.

Of course later on there were prom pictures taken on that porch, sidewalk chalk drawing masterpieces, and the flowers in bloom around the porch made for a great graduation picture. Over the years I've painted that porch a million times and always the same color. On that same porch I stood holding my very first paycheck as my Dad took the picture. I sold fresh lemonade for a nickel and repaired damaged kites there. I especially enjoyed laughing with my sister and mother over something stupid one of our men did. Occasionally a neighbor might see you out and come on over for a beer to catch up on the latest news down the street. Before you know it another couple comes over to show off their new car and then the BBQ gets lit and it's a party. Don't ya just love moments like that?

Yup, we take porches for granted. The history they see, the secrets they keep, the laughs they echo, the tears that soak them. So, "cheers" to the family front porch; may it weather all the times of our lives for generations to come.

~ ABOUT THE AUTHOR ~

Carol has had the burning desire to be a writer and artist since early childhood, working hard to achieve this life-long goal against many obstacles. She was raised in the quiet town of Montgomery, New York with her parents and three siblings and is the single mother of two children. After exploring the world, and getting a B.A. and M.A. from SUNY Fredonia in writing, she returned to the Hudson Valley settling in Pine Bush to enjoy spending time with her family.

Carol is mostly known for her popular "Smirk" humor column which she hopes will become syndicated in many more publications in the future. Her love of drawing and oil painting has enabled her to have several art shows of her works in various galleries and businesses through-out New York. Her hobbies include ghost hunting with her team of paranormal investigators, collecting colorful antique glass bottles, gardening, horseback riding, hiking, camping, and the list goes on...

With the help of her loyal fans her goal is to make this book a number one best seller hopefully opening more doors for her to continue her writing in other capacities. She has written three movie screenplays entitled, "Party Girls", "The Momz Club" and "Lizzie Borden", which have received awards in various screenplay competitions and are available for option. Her current projects in the works are a series of ten children's books, a book on her paranormal investigation experiences, and a second book of Smirk columns and illustrations. In the future she would like to explore comedy writing for a television sitcom, and producing her movies. If you would like your local newspaper to carry this weekly column urge them to do so by contacting the author at her web-site.

Check out Carol's Blog and other fun stuff at her web-site:
www.SmirkMe.com
Contact e-mail for Carol is: SmirkMe@gmail.com

I gratefully thank every person that has bought this book.

Consider yourself officially Smirk~i~fied!

CPSIA information can be obtained at www.ICGtesting.com
Printed in the USA
BVOW051148150213

313395BV00001B/8/P